WHAT EVERY PARENT SHOULD KNOW ABOUT EDUCATION

How knowing the facts can help your child succeed

WHAT EVERY PARENT SHOULD KNOW ABOUT EDUCATION

How knowing the facts can help your child succeed

Chris Atherton
and Stuart Kime

First published in 2021 by Critical Publishing Ltd

British Library Cataloguing in Publication Data
A CIP record for this book is available from the British Library

ISBN: 978-1-913063-13-9

This book is also available in the following e-book formats:
EPUB ISBN: 978-1-913063-15-3
Adobe e-book ISBN: 978-1-913063-16-0

Cover and text design by Out of House Limited

Project management by Newgen Publishing UK
Printed and bound in Great Britain by 4edge, Essex
Critical Publishing

3 Connaught Road
St Albans
AL3 5RX

www.criticalpublishing.com

Paper from responsible sources

CONTENTS

MEET THE AUTHORS

CHRIS ATHERTON

Chris Atherton is the Assistant Principal at Sir John Deane's College in Cheshire, where he leads on curriculum innovation. He is a classroom teacher with over 15 years' experience teaching English language and literature. In addition to his teaching work, he is a parent and a governor at a local primary school. He is also the author of *Assessment: Evidence-Based Teaching for Enquiring Teachers*. You can find him on Twitter at @csatherton.

STUART KIME

Stuart Kime is the Director of Education at Evidence Based Education (EBE) where he is responsible for the design and delivery of all online and blended learning programmes. He is a qualified teacher and his research interests focus on assessment, teachers' professional learning, and evaluation. Stuart is a Visiting International Professor in the Hector Research Institute for Education Sciences and Psychology at the Eberhard Karls University, Tübingen, and an Honorary Professor in the School of Education at Durham University. He formerly held a Policy Fellow post in the UK Government's Department for Education.

1. WHY SHOULD I LEARN MORE ABOUT EDUCATION?

Parents and the education debate

One of the unexpected side-effects of the COVID-19 pandemic has been to raise profound questions about our education system. As schools were shut, exams were cancelled and children were forced to study at home, many of the controversies and contradictions that exist in education have come bubbling to the surface in a very public way. Debates such as:

- What are schools for?
- How do we support all students to succeed?
- Are A levels and GCSEs the best ways of assessing our students?
- What role should schools play in developing citizens?
- Are children put under too much stress?

One group was made to think very hard about these questions – parents. Stuck at home with children, and with the burden of education suddenly thrust upon them, many parents realised they didn't have answers to vital questions about education.

This book has been written to answer those questions. It tackles some of the major debates within education by exploring the latest research and information and it will help you navigate the world of education with confidence. Now is a perfect time to explore these debates because the education sector has better answers than they have ever done before. In recent years an evidence-based education movement has supercharged the debate around education, as schools engage with a raft of new research from fields such as psychology and cognitive science. We increasingly know what techniques and strategies have the greatest impact on learning, and which common practices are actually ineffective. A new, evidence-based model of education is emerging which, it is hoped, may represent the best version of our education system yet. The aim of this book is to share those insights with you.

Question 1: How can parents help a child be successful in school?

The central message of this book is that children get the most out of school when their parents properly engage with the complexities of education. This means:

1. they should try to **understand how education works** so that they can make good choices and recognise good teaching when they see it;
2. they should approach their relationship with the school in a **collaborative** manner so that they are able to help the school deliver the best outcomes for their child.

BEING KNOWLEDGEABLE ABOUT EDUCATION

Parents naturally tend view their children's education through the lens of their own experiences of school. This approach is not without merit or logic, but there is a lot of new information out there since you were at school, new ideas and new approaches that may make your experience less useful as a guide for your child's education. By knowing the latest ideas about how education works, and why teachers are doing the things that they do, you can be a valuable ally to schools who are trying to make things better for your children. A knowledgeable parent takes time to learn:

- the culture and ethos of their child's school;
- the curriculum they are studying (the content and sequence of knowledge they are learning);
- the basic principles of how learning, memory and assessment work;
- how education may change as children progress through school;
- what specific learning disabilities are and how they work.

COLLABORATING WITH THE SCHOOL

A collaborative parent fundamentally sees the school as an ally and a leader in their child's education, rather than an adversary to be overcome. Parents whose children are most successful in school tend not to see the school as a foe. Instead, they are collaborative with the school in the sense that they:

- engage directly and positively with the child's teacher about their child's education;
- back up what the child is told in the classroom, particularly around behaviour and culture;
- establish a similar culture around learning at home and provide support and challenge where it is needed to help the child succeed.

There is no perfect parenting style, but when it comes to education the best default position is to be a collaborative parent, who has taken the time to understand what and how the school teaches.

Question 2: Do people who work in education agree on what good education looks like?

No, people involved in education do not agree what a good education looks like. Since the birth of modern education in the eighteenth century, there have been two fundamentally different conceptions of what education should look like. These two educational philosophies are called **progressivism** and **traditionalism** and they have had the greatest impact on the landscape of the education debate today. Ironically, many teachers on the ground would not recognise these terms. Most modern educational experiences combine both of them to some degree and most teachers fall somewhere between these two extremes in terms of their personal beliefs.

Traditionalists believe that traditional classroom practices (such as the teacher at the front leading the learning, classrooms with students sat listening, repetition, memorisation, practice) are the best tools we have discovered for teaching children. They view these practices as part of an ancient educational tradition, stretching back to ancient Greece, and then extending through the British grammar school and public school traditions. In contrast, the **progressive** philosophy of education is critical of these traditional practices, viewing them as outmoded and harmful when taken to excess. In the progressive model of learning, the child is naturally endowed with creativity and motivation to learn, and it is believed that this gift is easily harmed by those same traditionalist educational practices that, in their eyes, exist primarily to enforce conformity.

Table 1A Progressive versus traditional education beliefs

PROGRESSIVE BELIEFS	TRADITIONALIST BELIEFS
The child should set the agenda for learning and do most of the communication.	The teacher should set the agenda for learning and do most of the communication.
Student engagement is created by entertaining, stimulating lessons that defy tradition.	Student engagement is created by appropriate behaviour management and well-taught traditional lessons.
Traditional education practices harm the child because they destroy their natural creativity and curiosity.	Progressive educational practices are ineffective and harmful because they mistake engagement for learning and don't actually help children learn.
Effective learning is based upon student-led discovery of knowledge through collaboration, exploration and discussion.	Effective learning is based upon teacher-led cultivation of individual knowledge.
Classrooms should be primarily discursive, interactive places centred upon the students' need for discovery.	Classrooms should be primarily places where children are expected to follow the lead of the teacher in order to learn.

As the name suggests, traditionalist practices have always been around in some form or other as long as there have been schools, but they have only really become codified as a teaching philosophy in the modern era under the sustained attacks from progressivist thinkers. Progressivism has its roots in the Romantic movement of the eighteenth century, but really began to influence mainstream schooling in the late Victorian era and the early twentieth century.

In recent history, progressive education really began to exert a strong influence over the education system in the late 1970s, when it increasingly became the orthodox view in teacher training.

Since the late 1990s, there has been a resurgence of interest in techniques that would generally be considered 'traditionalist'. Increasingly, recent governments (most famously, the Conservative government under the direction of Secretary of State for Education, Michael Gove) have adopted policies that have taken education in a more traditionalist direction, despite continuing objections from progressive voices in the education community.

A similar tension exists between academia and government, with a strong progressive tradition in many university teacher training departments and a growing commitment to traditionalist methods in recent government policy. Most notably, many of the most prominent voices in education (and thus the ones you are most likely to have heard of) are strongly associated with one tradition or the other. Sir Ken Robinson, whose TED talk on education is the most-viewed talk of all time, was probably the most famous advocate for progressivism. Similarly, Katherine Birbalsingh, headteacher at the prominent traditionalist school, the Michaela Academy, is a high-profile advocate for traditionalist values.

IT IS TIME TO REVISIT WHAT YOU KNOW ABOUT EDUCATION

The continuum between these two educational traditions is the primary landscape of the education debate. The aim of this book is not to advocate that parents should adopt one position or the other, but instead to suggest a third way of understanding what makes a good education – through examining the research evidence. In the past 20 years, this approach has emerged and rapidly begun to grow. It is not necessarily seeking to replace the existing philosophies, but to subject them to the same sort of evidence-based scrutiny that might be expected in medicine or social science research.

This is one of the major reasons why schools may not look like the schools of your childhood. Increasingly schools have started to engage with the research evidence on topics such as memory, learning and assessment, and as of September 2019, some of these approaches have even become embedded in the latest Ofsted inspection guidelines. Organisations such as the Educational Endowment Foundation (EEF) have emerged, a government-funded charity committed to testing and sharing the evidence on educational practices. Similarly, grassroots teachers' organisations such as researchED have emerged to help share evidence-based practice. This is the educational world of today, one where the rise of evidence-based practice is challenging old orthodoxies, and where schools are working hard to make sense of the new reality.

Summary

The education debate has been dominated by the contrasting ideologies of progressivism and traditionalism, although neither tends to be used exclusively. Understanding these two positions is extremely useful for making sense of the education debate and for evaluating much of the writing and commentary on education. This book does not seek to advocate for either side, but instead aims to take you beyond these ideological positions by looking at the best evidence that is currently available.

Ask a teacher

David Grimmett is a teacher and school leader, who also blogs at https://tlideasblog. wordpress.com/ and tweets under the handle @daveg5478

When did you first encounter the terms *progressive* and *traditionalist*?

I came across the terms for the first time on Twitter, and it seemed a strange kind of contradiction in terms for me that those who were embracing new research around the science of learning were being characterised as 'trads' while those still in love with fun at all costs were the 'progressives'. (I've realised since that it's not quite as clear cut as that, of course!)

How would you characterise each of the two positions?

Traditional – interested in promoting the teaching and learning methods that have a growing weight of evidence behind them. They look at the long-term gains rather than the short-term 'wow factor' in lessons. The methods they are interested in are rooted in the science of how people actually learn, and are not always pretty: retrieval practice, direct instruction, repeated practice, skills drills, interleaving. Proponents can be characterised as sucking the life out of education.

Progressives are interested in engagement and the human element of teaching and learning above all else. Learning will hopefully happen somewhere along the way as young people will be motivated and interested in the invariably exciting lessons and dynamic teachers who will somehow put each person's individual learning needs first every time.

Do you consider yourself to be more progressive or traditionalist in your practice and why?

I see myself as 70 per cent traditionalist, 30 per cent progressive. Sadly, it took 11 years of my teaching career before I had my Road to Damascus moment and recognised that the 'traditional' method of embedding learning over time was the way forward. I found it inconceivable that I had never really stopped myself over the previous decade and considered how I could ensure that students have the best chance of actually learning this stuff I'm ploughing through each day!

Do you think there is any way the two positions can be reconciled?

I don't believe the 'trad' methods need to be necessarily dull. My Year 10s adore the starter recap retrieval practice quizzes I run at the start of lessons, and the competitive element I use is a big part of that – eg, those seven or eight students who get the highest score out of ten from the recap quiz get a reward. What's great is that it is often not just the prior high-attainers who get the top marks with these quizzes, it can be anyone who's been listening hard in class.

Equally, we've created board games based on our knowledge organisers, articulate challenges and more. My team are always coming up with interesting ways of making the mechanics of learning core material fun and creative, and I celebrate that. There's always time too in a module for a drama sketch, or a game, or a fun activity – let's nurture that spark still! That's why I'm holding on to my progressive 30 per cent, and working on how the two positions can be reconciled.

What do you think are the main effects of the progressive/traditionalist divide on schools themselves?

There is some resistance as the 2000s was so 'prog' led. I've seen teachers glaze over when I begin talking about the science of learning and more traditional methods of retaining information over time. However, I've also seen teachers almost do a little jig when you share that it's OK now to take time over explanations, and that talking to students from the front for more than ten mins is OK! 'Trad' stuff will still annoy some, and enthuse others, but when you put hard evidence of learning gains in front of the 'progs', they ultimately have to sit up and take notice in my view, or we're simply not going to raise the quality of learning and results.

I think there are many shades of grey, and I don't think you'll find many teachers who would deem themselves to be exclusively 100 per cent one side or the other. I think what is important is that within schools' continuing professional development (CPD), and within meetings, that both sides are discussed and that compromises can be reached in terms of the curriculum for schools (hopefully more in favour of trad stuff!).

What should parents know about the progressive/traditionalist divide before their children start school?

I don't think parents need to worry too much. At the end of the day, parents want their kids to be happy, have fun in school, but also have their learning effort rewarded in terms of retaining enough knowledge and skills to pass their exams, and go off into the world more competent young people. I think if the two schools of thought are acknowledged, then schools will achieve this.

I would just possibly make more parents aware of the benefits of extended, repeated practice, and study methods that will yield higher retention rates over time – eg, retrieval practice, self-quizzing, etc. Any good school should make this clear from Year 7, and then parents will be able to support this vital component, leading to long-term success from the 'trad' resurgence.

WHAT EVERY PARENT SHOULD KNOW ABOUT EDUCATION

Conclusion

The global pandemic has forced many parents to become aware of the debates within education. Schools have changed significantly in the past couple of decades and the classroom your child is in might not be the same as the one you left many years ago. While there has always been an ideological divide between progressive teaching methods and more traditional models of education, these methods have increasingly been tested through research and we now have a much better idea of what constitutes the 'best bets' in education. This book will help you navigate this new educational environment by helping you understand some of the key insights from the evidence base. It will help you become the well-informed and collaborative parent who is able to support their child and their school.

❖ What to talk about on parents' evening

- **Progressive, traditionalist or a blend of both?** Most schools won't be overtly progressive or traditionalist, and most will fall somewhere in the middle of the spectrum, with many not even recognising the terms in how they describe themselves. If you're interested in progressive models of education, ask about student-centred learning and creativity. If you want to check their traditionalist credentials, ask about their policies on things like homework, behaviour and how much practice they do.

- **Engagement with research?** Many schools that engage in evidence-based practice have **research leads** or similar roles, a practitioner whose job it is to link the school to the world of academic research. Similarly, you could ask about what books or studies have influenced the way they teach.

further reading

If you are interested in reading further about evidence-based education and the education debate, we recommend the following:

- » For a summary of progressive arguments about education, and a critique of traditionalist education practices, you should read *You, Your Child and School: Navigate Your Way to the Best Education* by Sir Ken Robinson and Lou Aronica (2018).

- » For a traditionalist critique of progressive education read *Progressively Worse: The Burden of Bad Ideas in British Schools* by Robert Peal (2014). For an explanation of traditionalism in action, read *Battle Hymn of the Tiger Teachers: The Michaela Way* by Katherine Birbalsingh and the staff of the Michaela Academy in London (2016).

» David Didau's *Making Kids Cleverer: A Manifesto for Closing the Education Gap* (2019) is a fascinating and impeccably researched manifesto for making acquiring knowledge the focus of education.

Bibliography

Birbalsingh, K (ed) (2016) *Battle Hymn of the Tiger Teachers: The Michaela Way*. Melton, Woodbridge: John Catt Educational Ltd.

Didau, D (2019) *Making Kids Cleverer: A Manifesto for Closing the Advantage Gap*. Carmarthen: Crown House Publishing Ltd.

Peal, R (2014) *Progressively Worse: The Burden of Bad Ideas in British Schools*. London: Civitas.

Robinson, S K and Aronica, L (2018) *You, Your Child and School: Navigate Your Way to the Best Education*. London: Allen Lane.

2. SCHOOL CHOICE

Key information about your choice of school

- Gathering a range of dependable viewpoints about schools you are considering is helpful.
- The type of school your child attends matters less than the quality of teaching and leadership.
- Relationships of trust and respect between students and teachers, and among students, are vital for effective teaching and learning.
- Well-managed behaviour is an important consideration in school choice.

Ultimately, the philosophical positions on education held by leaders and teachers in schools translate – directly or indirectly – into the day-to-day activities in classrooms and corridors. And, because each school is charged with making decisions in the best interests of the students they teach, each is different. So what should you look for? What really makes a difference?

Knowing what types of school are available to you, their similarities and differences, and what about them really seems to make a difference to children are the topics of this chapter. Understanding more about these things and knowing where to find dependable information to inform your school-choice decisions is the next step to take in understanding the education process and collaborating confidently with your child's teachers and school leaders.

In this chapter, we summarise the features of the most common school types, and see that research evidence indicates that the type of school itself – local authority primary, secondary academy or free school, for instance – seems to affect the education that children receive far less than two other key factors:

1. the quality of school leadership;
2. the quality of classroom teaching.

The so-called *Bananarama Principle* (coined by Professor Steve Higgins at Durham University) applies: to paraphrase, it's not what type of school you're in, it's what happens in your school... and that's what gets results. But 'what happens in your school' is difficult to observe or experience as a parent or carer of a prospective new pupil or student. So, as well as understanding more about school type, this chapter helps you to drill down into what happens in and around a school, and seek out the best 'fit and feel' for your child. To do so, we guide you through:

- bringing together and triangulating key pieces of information from sources such as the school's website and recent Ofsted reports;
- visiting schools and putting key questions to teachers and leaders;
- learning about and understanding the role a school plays in the community it serves;
- talking to governors or trustees about their plans for the school's future.

What are some of the most common questions about school choice?

1. What is 'school choice'?
2. What are the similarities and differences between the types of school available?
3. Why and how do schools select pupils?
4. How can Ofsted reports help inform school-choice decisions?
5. Where can I find good sources of dependable information about the schools I'm considering?

Question 1: What is 'school choice'?

The English education system has a variety of school types available (from privately owned to publicly funded, academies and free schools, single-sex and mixed, grammar schools and comprehensives), and deciphering the differences between them can be confusing to many parents. Too much choice can be overwhelming but the best way to deal with the confusion is to gather together some relevant and dependable information – a process that we'll look at in detail later on in the chapter.

School choice – in England at least – is about asserting your right to indicate a preference for your child to attend a particular school.

But 'indicating a preference' isn't the same as 'getting a place' in your first-choice school, so for the 93 per cent of children who attend state-funded schools, the next step in the process is for their highest *possible* school preference to be respected and acted upon.

GEOGRAPHICAL LOCATION AND SCHOOL CHOICE

Let's acknowledge that – wherever you are in the process of choosing a school – some of your choices have already been made. For reasons such as family and jobs, you live in a particular place. Maybe you chose to live there, maybe you didn't; but the unavoidable fact is that, for most people, where you live affects the choices of school available to you.

If you live in a densely populated area, there will be a greater number of schools closer by than if you live in a less densely populated area (for example, according to the Office for National Statistics website in 2020, many London boroughs have a population density greater than 10,000 people per square kilometre, while Northumberland has 64 per square kilometre). And while population density clearly has an effect, it's also interesting to consider the connection between school quality ratings and house prices.

Whether you live in an urban, rural or coastal area, there is also the relationship between school quality ratings and house prices to consider. Government statistics published in 2017 revealed that house prices close to the 10 per cent best-performing primary schools in England were 8 per cent higher than others in the area. In those areas closer to the 10 per cent best-performing non-selective secondary schools, house prices were 6.8 per cent higher.

Clearly, then, even before many parents think about a school for their child, some school-choice decisions have already been made. But this shouldn't be a cause of despair! Indeed, we would argue that it's helpful, here, to remember the Bananarama Principle, and understand that it's what happens in schools that really makes a difference. We know of many schools in challenging contexts and with low Ofsted ratings that are doing incredible things to serve the needs of their pupils, things that a prospective parent would only know about it they seek out dependable information from a range of sources.

Summary

While you have some choice in the school your child attends, factors such as where you live have already shaped it. As we'll see later, while research evidence indicates that no one school type is significantly better than another in terms of academic outcomes, what can make a difference is the quality of leadership and teaching.

Question 2: What are the similarities and differences between the types of school available?

The type of school your child attends generally matters much less than the quality of teaching and leadership, but it can be helpful to see some of the key differences and similarities between common types.

Schools in England can, broadly, be grouped into two categories: those that are state-funded and those that are privately funded (sometimes known as 'independent' or, confusingly, 'public' schools). State schools in England either are funded through the local authority, or get their funding directly from central government. Private schools, on the other hand, charge a fee for the education they provide, and this is often paid directly by parents, though in some cases bursaries and scholarships are available.

Table 2A Types of state-funded school in England

COMMUNITY SCHOOLS	FOUNDATION SCHOOLS AND VOLUNTARY SCHOOLS	ACADEMIES AND FREE SCHOOLS	GRAMMAR SCHOOLS
Traditionally known as 'local authority maintained schools'. They follow the national curriculum and are independent of any business or faith group.	Funded by the local authority but sometimes receive support from faith groups.	Funded by not-for-profit academy trusts. They operate outside of the local authority's control.	These may be run by the local authority, a foundation, or an academy trust.
These schools do not have selection tests for entry.	These schools do not have selection tests for entry.	These schools do not have selection tests for entry.	Grammar schools select their pupils using entrance tests of academic ability.

The first two columns in Table 2A describe schools with which most people will be familiar to some extent – many parents in England will have attended a local authority school of one kind or another. Academies, however, are a relatively new and significant development in England's education system, and so we turn our attention to them now.

ACADEMIES

Academies were originally introduced by the Labour government in 2002 as a 'remedial intervention' to improve the quality of education in so-called 'failing schools'. After the Conservative/ Liberal Democrat coalition government came into power in 2010, the number of academies began to rise dramatically. Studies into the effects of this new school type find that there has been little impact of academies per se on children's outcomes, although some positive effects have been found (schools rated as outstanding by Ofsted before they converted to being an academy between 2010 and 2014 saw increases of around one GCSE grade in two subjects, on average).

Unlike community schools, academies do not have to follow the national curriculum (the collection of subjects that children in primary schools and secondary schools learn, and the standards they should meet in them), but they do have to offer something of equal or greater depth and ambition that responds to what children attending the school know and can do: they must respond constructively to fill the gaps in knowledge and skill the children they teach have.

According to the Department for Education in England, 32 per cent of primary schools and 75 per cent of secondary schools are (at the time of writing) either academies or free schools, with over four million children attending them (about 2.5 million of these children are in secondary schools, while more than 1.6 million are primary school children, and those not accounted for in these figures attend special and alternative provision academies). Academies have grown in number, and it seems likely that this trend will continue in years to come.

Summary

There is a variety of different school types available in England, although where you live will affect which are actually available to you. School type itself seems to affect the education that children receive less than the quality of the teaching and leadership, so it is advisable to focus your attention on what happens in and around a school, more than what type it is.

Question 3: Why and how do schools select pupils?

Most schools don't select pupils. Some schools, however, do have selection procedures for pupil admission; later in this section, we'll briefly consider selection in the contexts of single-gender schools and private schools, but first we take a look at grammar schools.

At age 11, when children move from primary school to secondary school (after the end of Year 6), most go to a state-funded school which is non-selective. A small number go to one of the 163 academically selective **grammar schools** which use entrance testing to assess a child's achievement and ability. Their presence in the English education system stems from national and local policy decisions which have created heated debates about privilege, segregation and fairness in society. But these debates generally don't directly affect the majority of parents, due to the relatively small number of grammar schools in the country (which tend to be clustered in certain geographic regions – there is only one in Cumbria, for example, and 15 in Lincolnshire).

But what does the research evidence say about the selection of pupils into different schools? In 2008, a group of Durham University academics wrote a report for the Sutton Trust which looked at the evidence on the effects of selective education systems (Coe et al, 2008). The researchers set out what they saw as the arguments for and against selection, and these are summarised in Table 2B (using the authors' own words).

Table 2B Summary of arguments presented by Coe et al (2008) for and against selecting children to attend different schools

ARGUMENTS FOR SELECTION	ARGUMENTS AGAINST SELECTION
- It is appropriate for different types of pupil to have different kinds of education. - Teaching can best be targeted at a narrow ability range. - Grammar schools are meritocratic and socially redistributive by providing advantage for the bright but poor. - Grammar schools are socially inclusive, as they keep the middle classes in state education. - The academic elite should be a priority for education. - Grammar schools provide a beacon of excellence. - Grammar schools achieve better academic results. - Selection operates elsewhere within the educational system.	- Selection tests are never fair or adequate. - Ability is multidimensional and fluid. - The impact of failure on pupils not selected is unacceptable. - Selection has an adverse effect on the primary school curriculum. - Selection is socially divisive. - Selection compounds disadvantage. - It is the socially disadvantaged who should be a priority for education. - Selection limits parental choice. - Selective systems produce worse academic results.

There are arguments and opinions on either side of the debate around selection, and more recent research evidence on grammar schools published by Durham academics Stephen Gorard and Nadia Siddiqui concludes that there is little to support for the continued presence of grammar schools in the education system. Summarising their findings, the academics had this to say in their 2018 paper:

The policy is a bad one and, far from increasing selection, the evidence-informed way forwards would be to phase out the existing 163 grammar schools in England. This is not to decry the schools that are currently grammars, or the work of their staff. But, overall, they are simply no better or worse than the other schools in England once their selected and privileged intake is accounted for. There is no reason for them to exist.

(Gorard and Siddiqui, 2018)

The knowledge, skill and dedication of leaders and teachers in grammar schools is not to be diminished. But it is important to acknowledge the body of research indicating that this school type per se is not superior to any other, something that can also be said for single-gender schools.

SINGLE-GENDER SCHOOLS

If you are considering either an all-boys or all-girls school for your child, you may be surprised to find that – despite anecdotes and intuition – research suggests that sending your child to one appears to make very little – if any – difference to how well they're likely to do academically. This is not to say that they won't flourish in a single-gender school, but that, on average, this school type does not confer an academic advantage per se (yet again, the Bananarama Principle returns!).

Such findings are seen not just in England, but in several countries around the world. In 2014, researchers in the USA concluded that '*Results from the highest quality studies, then, do not support the view that SS* [single sex] *schooling provides benefits compared with CE* [co-educational] *schooling*' (Pahlke et al, 2014).

When we spoke to Durham University's Professor Stephen Gorard for this book, he offered his thoughts on why, for example, single-gender girls' schools seem to achieve better results than mixed-gender schools: '*Single-sex girls' schools have results in line with those of girls in mixed* [co-educational] *schools – they just have more girls so the average is higher as girls tend to have better outcomes.*' Looking at the research evidence, we have to conclude that attending a single-gender school appears to make very little – if any – difference to how well a child is likely to do academically (although clearly, this is only one consideration in the school-choice decision, albeit an important one).

Neither grammar schools nor single-gender schools seem to confer an academic advantage on the students who attend them, but what about private schools?

PRIVATE SCHOOLS

Defining private schools (sometimes known as 'independent' or – confusingly – 'public' schools) is not as simple as offering a neat, one-line description. As ever in the world of education, things are a little more complicated than that.

For example, the 1400 or so schools registered on the Independent Schools Council website (www.isc.co.uk/schools/) include day schools and boarding schools, co-educational schools and single-sex schools, faith schools and those with no religious affiliation. While private schools often have long histories and are well-known, the number of pupils attending them in England has gone down in recent years: there were 2300 fewer pupils attending in 2019 than in 2017 (Department for Education, 2019).

While entrance testing is common in many private schools, not all select children based on their ability (as demonstrated by performance on an entrance test, for instance), although paying school fees creates a form of selection for all but those who receive the (often generous) bursaries and scholarships available.

As with grammar schools and single-gender schools, research evidence indicates that attending a private school does not necessarily confer an academic advantage on average (Ndaji et al, 2016), but for those who *can* afford it, does it have an impact on other outcomes, such as careers and income later in life?

A 2019 report from the Sutton Trust and the Social Mobility Commission indicated that a disproportionate number of influential positions in public life (in politics, for instance) are dominated by those who attended private schools. Additionally, University College London's Francis Green wrote in 2019 that research evidence indicated a '*17 percentage point wage premium for privately educated alumni once they reach the age of 25*'. Green goes on to say that, '*If replicated at a later age, that is the sort of long-term advantage that can begin to warrant the "investment" that many rich parents choose to make*' (Green, 2019).

Summary

Some schools select students: by ability, by gender or financially. Many make the argument that characteristics of their school type - such as its basis for selection - lead to better academic outcomes for students, on average. But is this really the case? Mostly, the answer to this question is 'no', although there do seem to be other ways in which certain types of school confer certain advantages. In most cases, school type makes much less of a difference than the quality of teaching and leadership.

Question 4: How can Ofsted reports help inform school-choice decisions?

WHAT IS OFSTED?

Ofsted (the Office for Standards in Education, Children's Services and Skills) is an apolitical body that exists for children and young people (and, by extension, for parents). It is the regulatory organisation that inspects maintained schools and academies in England, some independent schools, and all other services which provide education and skills for learners (outside of higher education); they are also responsible for the inspection and regulation of children's and young people's care services. Ofsted is there to help parents by reporting on the quality of education children receive in schools, and whether children are appropriately safeguarded from the risk of neglect, abuse or harm.

READING OFSTED REPORTS

Ofsted inspections are intended to provide a first-hand, clear-eyed snapshot view of a group of educators (Ofsted school inspectors are all teachers or senior leaders) which leads to the

WHAT EVERY PARENT SHOULD KNOW ABOUT EDUCATION

publication of freely available reports on the organisation's website (www.gov.uk/government/organisations/ofsted); these are designed to summarise what has been observed in a school in a way that is accessible and useful to you. You can help inform your school-choice decisions by reading the reports for the schools you are considering.

The reports present inspection findings to help you decide where to send your child to school (or to press for something different in the school your child already attends if you believe that change is needed), and while it has often been considered fashionable to 'bash' Ofsted, the organisation plays an important role in helping to raise standards in the English education system: it can help you understand what the education in a school is really like and if the children there are safe. Similarly, in Wales, parents can turn to the regulator, Estyn (www.estyn.gov.wales/), and in Scotland to Education Scotland (https://education.gov.scot/education-scotland).

To understand more about what information provided by Ofsted can – and cannot – do for you, let's look at the process of an inspection.

THE 'CALL'

In schools, the phrase 'We've had the call' – signalling that an inspection is imminent – marks the beginning of an important process, and one that the school's teachers, leaders and governors will have spent significant time (often years) preparing for. Once it has been uttered, things tend to move pretty quickly.

Schools generally find out about an inspection the day before it begins, although Ofsted can inspect a school without any notice at all if that is deemed to be appropriate (for instance, if there is a serious safeguarding concern). This should offer you a degree of reassurance; you should expect that what is inspected is 'normal practice' and not something staged through weeks and weeks of pre-inspection rehearsal.

THE INSPECTION

On the day of the inspection, inspectors ask questions and review evidence in order to form a judgement about the school's overall effectiveness, as well as individual judgements in four key areas:

- the quality of education;
- behaviour and attitudes;
- personal development;
- leadership and management.

Once a range of relevant information has been collated and reviewed, inspectors use a four-point scale to indicate their judgement, based on all of the evidence that they have gathered:

- Grade 1 (Outstanding);
- Grade 2 (Good);
- Grade 3 (Requires improvement);
- Grade 4 (Inadequate).

Once an inspection visit is completed, a report will be written and published; the school must take every reasonable step to ensure that each parent of a child currently in the school receives a copy. For a prospective parent, it is one of the pieces of information that should be used to help inform your school-choice decisions (all published reports can be found at https://reports.ofsted.gov.uk/).

Whether an inspection visit itself can accurately capture the quality of education in a school is one matter; whether what is captured on the day can be accurately reported and communicated in a single written document is another altogether (if you've ever tried to relay accurately and completely the details of a holiday, a wedding, even a conversation at work, you'll know that it's hard to communicate every aspect of the experience). Now put yourself in the shoes of an inspector...

Ofsted inspectors see a lot more than could ever be communicated in a report (it would be unreadable if they wrote absolutely everything!); they write about the main things that they believe parents should read about. The reports are not a total description of the quality of a school, but they do pick out the things that parents both need and want to know.

DO OFSTED RATINGS REFLECT THE QUALITY OF EDUCATION MY CHILD WILL RECEIVE?

The simple answer to this question is 'no'. A school's Ofsted rating cannot accurately capture the quality of an entire school, nor can it tell you what will happen in the future. In reality, could any system of inspection accurately capture the quality of something as complex and dynamic as a school?

Ofsted inspection ratings and reports can only ever summarise certain aspects of what has happened *in the past* at a school (they're inspectors, not time travellers or soothsayers), so they're valuable as one of the sources of information you should use, but they can't predict the educational experience your child will have. As Stephen Gorard sees it, Ofsted ratings are '*mostly a reflection of school intakes*' and while they provide you with *one* important piece of the jigsaw puzzle, it is the **triangulation** of *lots* of pieces of dependable information that is most helpful in informing your school-choice decisions (something that we'll look at further later in this chapter).

Have a look at https://reports.ofsted.gov.uk/ to find the most recent reports for schools that you're considering (or, indeed, your child's current school). When you visit the school, ask how teachers and leaders have responded to its findings (what effect it had on their work, and what actions they have taken in light of it).

Summary

Ofsted reports offer one piece of information to help with your school-choice decision, but they may well have been published a number of years ago, and may no longer reflect the school as it currently is. Also, be cautious about the rating given to a school, as it can give only a very limited snapshot of the school.

Question 5: Where can I find good sources of dependable information about the schools I'm considering?

When you're looking for information – in addition to Ofsted reports – to help you decide on the right school for your child, where should you look? Academic results in subjects that matter most to your child, the school's website (especially details about the curriculum), and the views of current parents and those in the wider community should be on your list. Above all else, visit the school, talk to staff, governors and parents, and get a good feel for the place.

TRIANGULATE MULTIPLE VIEWPOINTS

Simply looking at the school's **academic results** in subject areas that matter most to your child is a good next step in building up the jigsaw puzzle of information you need (but remember that results achieved by other children in years gone by is not a prediction for how your child will do). While it's always difficult to say what has caused really great (or really not so great) results, looking at the trends over a few years is one way of getting a quick sense of how children in that school achieve – on average – in areas that are important to your child. But that's just one (fairly narrow) view of a school, and you'll need to go further than this to build a more complete picture.

When we spoke to Alex Quigley (former English teacher and now National Content Manager at the Education Endowment Foundation), he echoed the view that triangulating information from a number of dependable sources is a good approach to take in building your understanding of a school and its 'fit' for your child. Quigley suggests starting with a school's website and trying to get a feel for not just *what* goes on there, but *how* it goes on as well. For example, does the curriculum (outlining what your child will learn) seem rich and likely to spark *your* child's curiosity?

Once you've explored the website, try to find out how well the school engages with the local community; this is where you need to get out and about, talking to people who already have children in the school you're interested in. It can be hard to begin connecting with a network of people who know the school well, but the hard work pays off in the long-run. In many schools, Quigley says, '*the curriculum extends beyond the school gates*' in the form of additional programmes and events designed to serve the local community, so it's worth asking what is offered and what kinds of things you and your child could be involved in above and beyond the lessons that will be taught during the normal school day.

Gathering together what Quigley calls '*informal, local, community insights*,' and then combining these with information drawn from publications such as Ofsted reports (although even the most recent of these, Quigley cautions, may have been published several years ago) and website details should help you build a fuller picture of a school, but this is still probably not sufficient. Ultimately, the next step should be to visit the school and see if your child feels safe, supported and curious to learn.

ASK SCHOOL LEADERS AND TEACHERS ABOUT THE THINGS THAT REALLY MAKE A DIFFERENCE TO STUDENTS' LEARNING

We established earlier that the type of school matters less on average than what actually happens in a school. Remember the Bananarama Principle? Well, research on the effectiveness of teaching tells us that there are a few common influences on children's experiences in school that are most likely to have a positive effect on their education. And, because your child will spend more than a decade of their life in school, it's worth asking some questions about three key areas:

- **a supportive classroom environment;**
- **effective classroom management;**
- **cognitive activation (thinking hard about things to be learned).**

In later chapters, we'll look in detail at what teachers and leaders actually do in these areas, but for now, here are some brief summaries that will help you to focus your questions.

CREATING A SUPPORTIVE CLASSROOM ENVIRONMENT

In June 2020, Professor Rob Coe and colleagues published *The Great Teaching Toolkit: Evidence Review*, and said: '*A supportive classroom environment is characterised by relationships of trust and respect between students and teachers, and among students. It is one in which students are motivated, supported and challenged and have a positive attitude towards their learning.*'

Every child struggles to learn at some point (as we'll see later, struggling can be a *good* thing!), and the more supportive classroom environments help them through this by encouraging students to see the link between their own efforts and their successes (or failures). In a supportive classroom where students and teachers have positive relationships, children will know that their own actions are inherently linked to the outcomes they achieve.

The relationship between teachers and the children in their classes is one of the foundations of effective learning, so asking a prospective school how they foster strong, positive relationships in classrooms will give you a useful insight into an important aspect of your child's education. It's one of the pieces of information you should gather along your school-choice journey.

CLASSROOM MANAGEMENT

Teachers have very different styles, priorities and values in their teaching, but effective classrooms are ones in which the behaviour and activities of students are well-managed.

Alongside the supportive environment of effective classrooms in the school, well-managed classrooms have clearly and consistently enforced rules and routines. Intuitively, they might appear to some parents to stifle children's creativity and individuality, to constrain learning more than they enhance it. But schools are communities in which individuals learn and grow, and both the community and the individual benefit from a sense of reassurance and clarity that comes from appropriate rules-based systems.

Effective classroom teachers manage time and resources efficiently to maximise productive time and minimise time wasted; they ensure rules, expectations and consequences for behaviour are explicit and consistent; and they prevent, anticipate and respond to potentially (and actually!) disruptive incidents.

Research into effective classrooms also suggests that there is one other core component to consider when you're looking for the right school for your child: the extent to which they are encouraged and supported to think hard about the things they're learning.

GETTING STUDENTS TO THINK HARD

Classrooms in which children tend to learn effectively are ones in which they have to think hard about the topics in the curriculum they are following. For some, the idea of a 'cognitive struggle' is one that gets incorrectly translated as 'make it really hard for them', but this misses the point. Thinking hard about something can only be an effective learning tool if a child has the relevant prior knowledge to attempt something more challenging (like a new tense in a foreign language), and if they are in an environment that is supportive (failure is a common product of trying new, more challenging things, so being able to 'fail well' is important). In good classrooms, teachers know how to engineer situations that engage students' curiosity as a means to generate cognitive activation, rather than simply setting lots of very hard problems for them to solve.

Summary

Predicting the quality of education that your child is going to experience is a bit like predicting the weather, albeit less accurate. By triangulating information from Ofsted reports, schools' websites, current parents and school visits (where you can have conversations about how they create supportive, well-managed classrooms in which children think hard about their learning), you can increase your confidence that the school choice you're making is the right one.

Conclusion

A lot of school choice is about the 'feel and fit' of a school for your child: what matters is what teachers, leaders, governors and students do and the way that they do it. Inspection reports are indispensable as a source of information, but they – like all of the other pieces of the jigsaw puzzle from academic results, a school's website, other parents' views and how your child responds when you visit a school – are small, fragmented parts of the full picture needed to help you make the best decision you can.

❖ What to talk about on parents' evening

With the inspection reports read, the website visited, and conversations with existing parents or others who know the school well, visit the school and consider discussing these points with teachers and leaders.

- **Fit and feel.** Have a conversation with teachers and school leaders about things that your child is really interested in. Ask them how they would support these passions and interests, and what they would do to ensure that your child has a really broad and balanced education. And crucially, ask your child what they think about the school.

- **School improvement plans.** Talk to the school's leaders about their last inspection report. Ask them what the report indicated were the key areas for improvement, and what the school has done in response. This should give you an idea about how the school's development plans are going, and what plans are in the pipeline.

- **Rules and routines.** Find out about how teachers in the class that your child would enter manage their classes. Ask about the rules and routines that are used to help maximise learning, and what you as a parent could do to reinforce and support these at home.

further reading

To find out more about some of the topics covered in this chapter, here are some suggestions for further reading:

» *The Great Teaching Toolkit: Evidence Review* by Rob Coe, C J Rauch, Stuart Kime and Dan Singleton (2020) provides an accessible insight into what the best available research evidence says about effective teaching.

» *Seven Myths About Education* is a thought-provoking book about teaching. The author, Daisy Christodoulou, looks at seven widely held beliefs and practices in education that she believes are holding back students and teachers.

Bibliography

Christodoulou, D (2014) *Seven Myths About Education*. London: Routledge.

Coe, R, Jones, K, Searle, J, Kokotsaki, D, Kosnin, A M and Skinner, P (2008) *Evidence on the Effects of Selective Educational Systems: A Report for The Sutton Trust*. Durham: CEM Centre, Durham University.

Coe, R, Raunch, C J, Kime, S and Singleton, D (2020) *The Great Teaching Toolkit: Evidence Review*. [online] Available at: www.greatteaching.com (accessed 15 February 2021).

Department for Education (2019) Schools, Pupils and their Characteristics. [online] Available at: https://assets.publishing.service.gov.uk/government/uploads/system/uploads/attachment_data/file/812539/Schools_Pupils_and_their_Characteristics_2019_Main_Text.pdf (accessed 15 February 2021).

Gorard, S and Siddiqui, N (2018) Grammar Schools in England: A New Analysis of Social Segregation and Academic Outcomes. *British Journal of Sociology of Education*, 39(7): 909–24.

Green, F (2019) Getting the Science Straight: The Schools Minister's Suggestion that Private Schools Convey Little Academic Advantage Does Not Stand Up to Scrutiny. [online] Available at: https://ioelondonblog.wordpress.com/2019/07/09/getting-the-science-straight-the-schools-ministers-suggestion-that-private-schools-convey-little-academic-advantage-does-not-stand-up-to-scrutiny/ (accessed 15 February 2021).

Ndaji, F, Little, J and Coe, R (2016) *A Comparison of Academic Achievement in Independent and State Schools*. Durham: CEM Centre, Durham University.

Pahlke, E, Hyde, J S and Allison, C M (2014) The Effects of Single-Sex Compared with Coeducational Schooling on Students' Performance and Attitudes: A Meta-Analysis. *Psychological Bulletin*, 140(4): 1042–72.

Sutton Trust and Social Mobility Commission (2019) Elitist Britain 2019. [online] Available at: www.suttontrust.com/wp-content/uploads/2019/12/Elitist-Britain-2019.pdf (accessed 15 February 2021).

3. LEARNING

Key information

- Learning is a process, not an event. It takes place over time and requires extensive revision and reinforcement.
- Skills cannot easily be separated from knowledge, and the best methods for improving skills involve deliberate practice and improving knowledge.
- While learners vary enormously, it is a mistake to think we have distinct learning styles that must be catered for.
- Teachers don't teach in laboratory conditions and lots of cultural or environmental factors can impact learning.

What do you need to know about how we learn?

1. Why haven't we learnt something once we've experienced it?
2. How does memory work?
3. Are skills more important than knowledge?
4. Do we all learn in different ways?

Question 1: Why haven't we learnt something once we've experienced it?

A common misconception about the learning process is that once we have experienced and engaged with new material, we have learnt it. This makes intuitive sense because we often feel like we know more about something immediately after we've experienced it – students tend to feel confident they know something after they have covered it in class. But the reality is that merely experiencing something isn't the same as learning.

Your memory is unreliable. We struggle to retain the entirety of anything we have experienced. However, in the case of most learning, the problem is much more fundamental than retention. The problem lies in the relationship between memory and thought. As the psychologist Daniel Willingham has described it, 'memory is the residue of thought' (Willingham, 2008a, p. 1). Without thought we don't create memory, and without memory there can be no learning. Many things that seem like learning – sitting in a lecture theatre listening to someone talk, watching a YouTube video, even reading an article – don't automatically force you to think in relevant ways, and therefore don't necessarily lead to a change in memory.

Schools need to be careful that they don't assume that just because a child is present in a class they are automatically learning. Disengagement from thinking, or a poorly designed learning task, can create an environment in which very little thinking is taking place. Similarly, teachers should beware of activities that create the wrong kinds of thought and learning for the aims of the lesson. If a child is asked to colour in a picture of Henry VIII, this may be highly stimulating, and the child may love doing it, but will they actually learn anything about Henry VIII? Engagement isn't the same thing as learning.

Summary

Unless it creates relevant thought, exposure to new material or engagement are not enough by themselves to create learning. As a result, a lot of things that look and feel a lot like learning might not actually have much learning in them at all.

Question 2: How does memory work?

A useful definition of learning might be that one used by Peps Mccrea, Dean of the Institute of Teaching. In a recent paper he defines learning as '*a persistent change in knowledge*' (Mccrea, 2018, p. 25). The key word here is 'persistent'. Comprehension at one point in the learning process does not guarantee learning in the longer term. Imagine a student in a maths class is told how to solve a new type of equation. The student listens to the teacher explain how to solve these new sums and then they successfully complete a couple of examples in their exercise book. Both the teacher and the student could be forgiven for assuming that the student has now learnt this new type of equation. But will the student still know how to complete that type of sum the next day? In a week? In ten years?

WORKING AND LONG-TERM MEMORY

We've known since the work of Hermann Ebbinghaus in 1885 that memory rapidly fades over time. Learning is not something that is complete once initial comprehension has taken place; just because I 'get it' in the classroom, it doesn't mean I've learnt it. It takes repeated exposure, comprehension and application to begin to construct the durable and effective memories we might call 'learning'. There are actually two different kinds of memory involved when we learn something. The first is what is called **working memory**. This is the everyday processing power we use to negotiate the world around us. When we are walking, talking, listening and thinking, it is working memory that we use to process the world as we experience it. But working memory is the gateway that knowledge must pass through to reach a second type of memory known as **long-term memory**. This is the persistent store of knowledge we build up through learning.

Table 3A Working and long-term memory

WORKING MEMORY	LONG-TERM MEMORY
Processes immediate experience. Limited. Resource-heavy to use.	Is drawn upon by working memory. Vast. Doesn't consume significant resources to use.

For something to be a *persistent* change in knowledge it must have passed from working memory to long-term memory. This is a surprisingly difficult process for several reasons.

- Memory fades rapidly after being established.
- The act of forming memories is hard work for the student and something they may actively avoid if they can.
- Working memory is limited and therefore can only pass so much through to your long-term memory at any one time.

Studies have shown that one of the most effective methods for transferring knowledge from working memory to long-term memory is a process called **retrieval practice**. This is the process of repeatedly quizzing yourself (or being quizzed), calling something up from memory time after time until the brain firmly secures it in long-term memory. This is as opposed to the belief in learning by exposure outlined earlier, which assumes that just by being exposed to the information our brains secure it in memory.

The other key factor to be aware of about memory is the phenomenon called **cognitive load**. The limited nature of working memory means that our brains can only handle so much information at once. This puts constraints on how quickly a child can learn, and has also revealed teaching strategies to support children to learn. Imagine a child's working memory as a narrow bridge over which learning must pass to reach their long-term memory and become 'learnt'. If the passage of information across the bridge is not carefully managed, the bridge can become overloaded and collapse. Similarly, if you don't make efficient use of the bridge, passing little across it, insufficient learning will cross to allow the child to assemble the idea properly on the other side. Effective learning should aim for a sort of Goldilocks effect – not easy, but not so hard it overloads the brain either. This has huge implications for how learning activities are designed. Teachers must manage working memory resources carefully and they can do this by:

- minimising distractions, so brain power isn't wasted on frivolous things;
- 'scaffolding' tasks – making them more manageable by providing detailed instructions, model answers and guidance;
- carefully teaching students in sequence to build up understanding.

Summary

The learning process takes place over a long period of time, and is a persistent change in knowledge, meaning that learning affects long-term memory, not just working memory. It takes more than comprehension to commit knowledge to long-term memory and consider something learnt. One of the most effective processes for establishing it in long-term memory is retrieval practice, and repeated exposure to material is not enough by itself. Once understanding is secured in long-term memory, students need to continue using it and applying their understanding to make it versatile enough to be used in new contexts. Good teachers also need to carefully manage the effort of learning to make sure students are working hard enough without becoming overwhelmed.

Question 3: Are skills more important than knowledge?

One prominent idea in the modern education debate is the idea that skills have become more important than knowledge. The economists Frank Levy and Richard Murnane famously claimed that traditional academic subjects should no longer be the focus of the academic process and instead the goal should be to cultivate new cross-disciplinary generic skills, called twenty-first-century skills, that will allow the child to adapt to whatever role or challenge they encounter in the adult world of work (Levy and Murnane, 2012). These twenty-first-century skills include:

- critical thinking;
- creativity;
- problem-solving;
- digital literacy.

This argument depends upon a clear distinction between skills and knowledge. It suggests that traditional academic knowledge has become less important in the modern age. Indeed, some versions of the argument insist that skills can be taught independently of knowledge. Why should children learn things when they can just Google them? The Indian educationalist Sugata Mitra, whose experiments with computer terminals in an Indian slum inspired the film *Slumdog Millionaire*, thinks that knowledge itself is irrelevant, arguing that in an internet age we no longer need to learn facts like we did in the past. Similar arguments have been made by public figures as diverse as Sir Richard Branson, Bill Gates and Jeff Bezos. In these arguments, skills and knowledge are decoupled completely, and those that will be successful are those that have been trained in generic literacies that can then make use of the easy access to knowledge that technology has provided.

WHY KNOWLEDGE MATTERS

Psychologists André Tricot and John Sweller (2014) have raised a significant obstacle to this model of learning. They argue that the problem with abstract skills such as critical thinking or problem-solving is that they are not really abstract skills. The argument for teaching generic skills rests on the claim that if you practise problem-solving in maths (eg, calculating the size of a sphere) it will in some sense build a general problem-solving skill that will be useful when you solve a problem in history (eg, determining the causes of the American Civil War). In actual fact, your ability to be creative or solve problems is mainly restricted to the domains of knowledge you have mastery of. If you learn how to solve problems in maths, you are only really becoming better at maths problem-solving. If Tricot and Sweller are right, then skills are intrinsically bound up with knowledge. By cultivating knowledge in a particular domain we grow the mental structures we need to practise skills effectively in that domain. Take architecture, for example. Most people could probably come up with a rough sketch for a new building, but it takes thousands of hours of mastering the domain of architecture, with all the maths, knowledge of materials and artistic practice, to be able to create one that could actually be built in the real world.

It is not that general problem-solving or general creative skill doesn't exist. People with naturally high intelligence tend to be better problem-solvers in all areas, indicating that problem-solving is, to some extent, a general skill. The issue is that it is very hard for teachers to improve general intelligence or generic skills and thus improve these skills. However, they *can* improve children's abilities within specific domains by teaching them knowledge within that particular domain. David Didau (2019) has made the argument that this approach is not only more effective, but it is also the moral choice *because* it is effective. By focusing on teaching knowledge well, we can actually improve children's intellectual skills, make them cleverer and give them better lives.

HOW SHOULD WE LEARN SKILLS?

You may already have heard of the *10,000-hour rule*. This was the central idea of Malcolm Gladwell's 2008 bestseller *Outliers*, which argued that unusually successful people were usually not produced by talent, but through extensive practice. Gladwell's central claim was that it takes roughly 10,000 hours to become proficient in any skill. This is an appealingly intuitive (and suspiciously round) number, but sadly it is wrong. The exact amount of practice required for proficiency can vary significantly depending upon what is being learnt. This is not to say that Gladwell is completely mistaken, however. Gladwell based his ideas upon the work of Anders Ericsson, a Swedish psychologist whose research has suggested that practice plays a much larger role in individual success than we originally thought.

Ericsson's research looked at what made experts successful in different fields. The studies he draws upon have looked at chess masters, elite athletes and virtuoso musicians, and his main conclusion is that it is what he calls **deliberate practice** that separates the highest performers from the rest, not intelligence or talent. When Ericsson talks about deliberate practice, he means a very specific set of conditions of practice.

- Practice should be **purposeful** – a student must have a clear outcome in mind and they must be consciously focusing on improving towards that outcome.
- Practice should be **guided by an expert**.

The main criticism of Ericsson's research is that it overstates the power of deliberate practice. One subsequent review of Ericsson's work published in the journal *Frontiers in Psychology* (Hambrick et al, 2007) suggested that the effect of deliberate practice only accounted for a third of the performance of elites in any given field. As many commentators have pointed out, deliberate practice is still constrained by inherent genetic abilities. If you're four feet tall, it's likely that no amount of deliberate practice will permit you to dunk a basketball.

Even if the case for deliberate practice is slightly exaggerated, the research still points to a much greater role for deliberate practice in academic success than many people had assumed. Very often, parents and schools frame learning as the unlocking of innate talent, but Ericsson's work suggests that mastery is something within the reach of almost anyone, given the right conditions of practice. It may impact how a school might think about things like ability groupings and target setting. It certainly goes against the idea that we should set artificial limits on what we assume a student is capable of. Most importantly, it affects how schools approach the learning process. Good teaching should make space for deliberate practice to build from knowledge into skill, instead of assuming that children learn through exposure to the information alone. If we want a child to acquire, say, good literacy skills, over the course of their education they must spend a large amount of time practising writing, with relevant instruction and feedback from teachers. The volume and duration of this practice is likely to be far greater than many people have traditionally assumed.

Summary

A foundation of knowledge is necessary for skills to grow and attempts to decouple skills and knowledge can be misguided. In particular, the belief that children should learn generic 'twenty-first-century skills' does not seem to fit the evidence. The best route to children acquiring academic or creative skills is probably through a combination of developing relevant knowledge and deliberate practice.

Question 4: Do we all learn in different ways?

One of the most persistent assumptions people make about learning is that every student learns in their own way and that if we fail to tailor learning to fit the individual, we can end up unfairly judging them to be a failure. One popular expression of these beliefs is what educationalists have called **learning styles**. This is the argument that children have individual biases in the way that they learn that correspond to different ways of learning. This theory argues that educators should know the learning preferences of their individual students and tailor this learning to their individual learning styles. Students who are not presented with information in a way that fits their learning style will be disadvantaged. There have been many versions of these learning styles over the years, but the one you are most likely to encounter is called VAK learning styles.

Table 3B VAK learning styles

TYPE OF LEARNER	DEFINITION
Visual learner	Learns primarily through seeing things. Teachers should use visualisations, images, diagrams to teach these.
Auditory learner	Learns primarily through hearing. Teachers should use discussion and oral explanation to teach these.
Kinaesthetic learner	Learns primarily through physical experience. Teachers should encourage physical interaction, use physical models and make physical representations to teach these.

The notion of learning styles is probably one of the most thoroughly debunked educational myths, yet it still persists in many educational environments. The problem with the idea of learning styles is this: fundamentally, maths must be learnt... as maths. If I am told I am a kinaesthetic learner and I learn a little dance that claims to teach the five times table, what I am primarily learning is the dance, not maths. It is true that if I watch a video of an African country in a geography class, this will help me to understand what life in one part of Africa looks like. This is because knowing what life in Africa looks like is visual information. I can't use the same technique to help me learn things that are not visual, such as the GDP of each country. Similarly, a child may have a particular set of skills that make them good at learning kinaesthetic information (they might be, say, a naturally proficient dancer), but if the knowledge in the subject is not itself kinaesthetic then they can't use that natural skill to learn that subject more effectively. Worse still, a child who is told they have a learning style will be encouraged not to cultivate or use their skills in other learning modes and will likely learn less than their peers.

SURELY YOU'RE NOT SUGGESTING THAT ALL STUDENTS ARE IDENTICAL?

Isn't it a good thing if teachers are attentive to the individual needs of students?

Of course teachers need to be sensitive to the needs of individuals, but there is a difference between acknowledging variance and expecting each learner to be completely unique or fit in a box. Human cognition does have common structures and processes and teachers must understand these to teach effectively. Learning styles are dangerous because they propose false structures and processes for learning. This is not to say that human cognition is the *only* factor that matters or that children's needs are identical, just that the underlying cognitive mechanisms for learning are fundamentally the same for almost all children.

Summary

There is no good evidence to support the claim that learning styles exist. Learning differences between children do exist, but unless they are associated with very specific learning disabilities, teachers should not try to excessively vary learning to accommodate them.

Ask an expert

Nick Rose worked as a postgraduate researcher in psychology before he joined teaching in 2003. He taught science and later psychology in secondary schools, eventually becoming a Leading Practitioner for Psychology and Research. He created the blog *Evidence into Practice* and co-authored (with David Didau) *What Every Teacher Needs to Know About Psychology*, published in July 2016. After working with TeachFirst as a research specialist between 2016 and 2018, he now works for Ambition Institute where he is involved in helping to design the Expert Teaching Masters programme.

What do we know about learning and memory that we didn't know 20 years ago and how is this changing what teachers do in the classroom?

It's interesting to see teachers are starting to engage with the science of learning – some of it isn't new! The fact that we quickly start to forget new learning can be a source of frustration for pupils (and their teachers!). However, the science tells us that memories that are forgotten are not lost. When we return to material, we relearn it quicker and retain it for longer each time. After a number of opportunities to return to the learning, we eventually find we have committed it 'to heart.'

Learning is never wasted – even when we appear to forget it. I think this is a really important finding – especially given how many of us think we have a poor memory. Even when we think something's forgotten, there's a trace in there somewhere that we can rekindle and consolidate. Even more positive than this, according to the psychologists Robert and Elizabeth Bjork, the fact that we forget may actually help us to learn!

The way memory appears to work means that when we have new learning fresh in mind – facts at our fingertips – then things like revision or restudy tend to be less effective. We actually need to forget – a little bit – to get the most benefit from returning to material we want to learn. This is useful for teachers because it can help inform the best ways to consolidate learning in long-term memory.

Testing ourselves is a highly effective way to reduce the amount we forget over time. As a consequence of this, teachers will often use informal quizzes and tests based on material pupils might have covered weeks or months previously. The best result is where we struggle to remember something (ie, we've forgotten it a bit), but with effort eventually retrieve it from memory. Not only does this help consolidate the memory – but it also helps us to make better judgements about what we really *know* and what we don't know, and therefore what we need to revise.

Why is acquiring knowledge so important to the learning process? Can't students just Google what they need?

If you were feeling very unwell, you'd seek out the expertise of a qualified doctor whose knowledge of medicine and the symptoms that indicate one type of illness from another allows them to diagnose what's ailing you and prescribe appropriate treatment. That doctor's knowledge, invaluable in medicine, won't be that useful if you have a problem with your car. A mechanic would have the knowledge to solve that problem, but likely wouldn't be the best person to consult if you're suffering chest pains.

Could the car mechanic simply look up your symptoms online and diagnose your illness? Well, possibly – I'm not sure I'd bet my life on their answer! In fact, knowledge helps you to know what to search for and, perhaps most importantly, what the results of the search mean. Even something as simple as looking up a word in an online dictionary benefits from having some background knowledge.

One dictionary.com definition of the word 'walk' is 'move by advancing the feet alternately so that there is always one foot on the ground in bipedal locomotion and two or more feet on the ground in quadrupedal locomotion.' *It actually requires quite a bit of knowledge to make sense of that definition – 'advancing,' 'alternately,' 'bipedal,' 'locomotion,' etc.*

So, it feels intuitively plausible that in an age where the world reference libraries can be accessed via a mobile phone, that 'knowing' has become obsolete – but the science appears to suggest that it's completely wrong. The evidence suggests that prior learning – what we know – is essential. To paraphrase Daniel Willingham, professor of psychology at the University of Virginia in the US: Knowledge isn't simply something we think about, *it's also what we think* with.

What is cognitive load theory and how has this had an impact on how teachers think about learning?

We've discussed the limited capacity of working memory – that it can only 'juggle' about four 'chunks' of information in mind at once. Cognitive load theory, developed by the educational psychologist John Sweller, argues that teachers need to consider this limited capacity when teaching their pupils – as a range of factors can make the 'cognitive load' placed on working memory too high – it can make the mental 'juggling act' too difficult for them. As a teacher, if I make too much of a demand on working memory, the pupil won't take much in (like trying to juggle too many balls at once – they will drop them!). Our working memory – our capacity to 'juggle' new information – is very limited and if we (as teachers) make too much demand on it (impose too high a 'cognitive load') our pupils will likely fail to learn very much in a lesson.

John Sweller's theory suggests that different aspects of the learning task and the environment place different 'loads' on working memory. For example, if I'm teaching a lesson in physics – perhaps looking at the flow of electrical current in different arrangements of circuits – then I'm potentially asking my pupils to 'juggle' several ideas at once. This means I need to consider a range of things in order to manage the 'cognitive load' I'm putting on working memory.

First – and most importantly – I need to know what my pupils already know about electricity and circuits: If they know quite a bit already and they are very familiar with the components of electrical circuits then that knowledge in long-term memory will help to 'chunk' larger amounts of information together, and I can set more challenging problems which will encourage them to think hard about the new learning. On the other hand, if they know next to nothing, then the 'size' of these 'chunks' is very small – and I'll need to really break down the learning and introduce new ideas step-by-step with examples and practice at each step, otherwise the 'load' I'm putting on their working memory might be too high.

Second, I should consider how abstract the material is. Some things are simply easier to visualise or hold in mind than others. If I'm asking pupils to think about something as abstract as 'packets of charge' moving (invisibly) through a metal wire, and that the number of these 'packets' passing any point on the wire every second is measured as Amperes... well, that's likely to be quite hard if they've never encountered these ideas before. Typically, our brains have evolved to cope well 'juggling' everyday objects and problems – like dividing up a pizza between friends or spotting when a friend has taken a slice of pizza they weren't supposed to have! However, much of the learning encountered in schools is not this everyday kind of knowledge – indeed, one reason we send children to school is to learn about this 'hard stuff' and we rely on the expertise of teachers to be good at teaching it (as any parent ambushed with a question like 'why is the moon?' may attest!).

I'll also need to consider how much loading on working memory is generated by the way that I teach the lesson. For example, it used to be something of a fashion in education to encourage pupils to discover ideas for themselves rather than explicitly teach them. The idea was attractive – in that I might arrange a practical activity (lots of wires, battery cells, circuit boards, lightbulbs and switches, etc) and lead pupils to discover that current varies in different arrangements of circuits by investigating the brightness of the bulbs. Indeed, I've tried teaching electrical current this way when I started teaching and the result was a lot of very confused pupils, who ended the lesson not really understanding very much about electrical current.

The problem was that I was asking them to 'juggle' too many things in their minds at once – not only the science, but also the equipment, getting the circuits built correctly, recording the results, working out what they meant, and so on. The evidence suggests that where pupils have relatively little knowledge and especially where the topic is quite abstract, it's better to break things down, step-by-step, with examples and practice at each step. This method of 'explicit teaching' helps to manage the cognitive load on working memory, by only introducing one or two new 'balls to juggle' at any stage (rather than throwing a whole basket of them at once!).

I'd also need to consider the environment of the classroom. Again, in a practical science lesson there are a whole host of distractions which add to the cognitive load but aren't related to the actual topic. Negotiating over circuit components, chatting with friends, losing your pen, working out whether the bulb is broken or the battery cell is flat... all of these things occupy space in working memory and may mean that the science doesn't really get a look in!

Lastly, the reason I'm carefully managing the load on working memory is that I want some capacity left over to think really hard about electrical current in a circuit. If their working memory is loaded up with other 'stuff' then there's not much room to really think about the science – and that means little knowledge will be laid down in long-term memory. As my pupils become more familiar with the abstract ideas, I can open up the lesson to different kinds of problems – including practical or investigation work – but if I try to do that too soon, they might enjoy it, but there's a good chance they won't understand very much. Indeed, they'll likely enjoy the practical elements of science a lot more once they have the foggiest about what's going on!

To what extent do children vary in the way they learn and why is it dangerous to think in terms of learning styles?

People vary in more ways than we can count – and teachers appreciate just as much as parents how each pupil is unique. However, there's also a great deal that people have in common – and that's usually the best place to start when thinking about learning. We all have a long-term memory – but we'll forget some things faster than others, and remember random things that other people forget. Some people have a better memory than others, but we all benefit from prior knowledge when learning new related topics, and we'll all forget less if we have the opportunity to try to retrieve things from memory over time. We all have a working memory – but that capacity changes rapidly over early childhood and some people will have more capacity than others. However, everyone's working memory is limited and benefits from having knowledge in long-term memory to support it and having a teacher who breaks things down when learning new things.

Indeed, knowing how memory and learning works for most people helps us understand these individual differences and how best to accommodate them. Many children will have special educational needs or disabilities related to learning, and often these will relate to things like working memory function or the rate at which new learning is consolidated in long-term memory. Many of the strategies teachers use to help pupils with special educational needs – breaking things down into smaller steps, modelling and carefully explaining steps and giving opportunities for practice and retrieving information before moving on to the next step – actually turn out to be really effective for all pupils!

However, it is true that some unhelpful ideas have grown up around individual differences in learning. One of these is the idea that people have particular 'learning styles' – and that teachers should try to match lesson activities to these styles.

However, while the idea might be intuitively appealing, the evidence simply doesn't support the idea of matching lessons to learning styles and in some cases the approaches to teaching suggested were genuinely unhelpful! We all have preferences about the way we learn – but it turns out that trying to match teaching to these preferences doesn't actually help. For example, we use all of our senses when learning – and a teacher would be well advised to use a diagram alongside their explanation for all children. Imagine trying to explain the shape of an Egyptian pyramid without the aid of a picture – regardless of whether someone might prefer to listen to things, it will be much easier to communicate the idea with an image!

Worse still, in some instances the idea of learning styles came to affect the confidence of pupils. I remember a sixth form student coming up to their A level exams deeply worried that they couldn't pass because they were a 'visual learner' and therefore not able to learn much from the textbook.

This is why research evidence is so important in teaching. You wouldn't expect to go to the doctor with a chest infection and have them recommend leeches – likewise, modern educators have an ethical duty to base their teaching on the best available evidence, rather than fads and fashions which might circulate in wider society.

Conclusion

Learning is a complex process that takes place over time, requires repeated practice and is difficult to capture or measure. Learning is more than just engagement or comprehension and it requires students to build detailed structures of knowledge in their long-term memory and regularly practise using them. It is easy to confuse learning with other things, such as engagement or scores on a test. Teachers should avoid unnecessary distractions or irrelevant thinking and carefully manage the complexity of learning in the classroom. To develop skills, schools should focus on providing environments where children are challenged to master academic or creative domains as effectively as possible through knowledge and practice.

❖ What should I talk about on parents' evening?

- **Revisiting learning and developing memory.** Discuss their approaches to making sure students have secured knowledge in memory. How they get students to learn key information? How (and how often) do students revisit learning from previous lessons? How do they make sure the students are thinking hard in your lessons?

- **Learning styles.** The use of learning styles in a school is a genuine concern and probably needs to be addressed directly. There are lots of good resources available (this book included) which you can use to support your claims. There is a particularly excellent

YouTube explainer by psychologist Daniel Willingham titled 'Learning Styles Don't Exist' (2008b).

- **Skills and knowledge.** You can better understand how they approach skills and knowledge by asking about specific skills such as maths and literacy. Ask about how they view the relationship between the knowledge they teach and the wider skills they hope to develop. Do they assess progress in skills and knowledge separately? How do students turn knowledge into skill?

further reading

The following books will really help if you want to find out more about the research into learning:

» Daniel Willingham's excellent book *Why Don't Students Like School? A Cognitive Scientist Answers Questions About How the Mind Works and What It Means for the Classroom* (2010) is an excellent read if you want to know more about the science of learning.

» *Understanding How We Learn* (2018) by Yana Weinstein and Megan Sumeracki is a bright visual guide to the science of learning with excellent illustrations. It makes even difficult concepts easy to understand.

Bibliography

Didau, D (2019) *Making Kids Cleverer: A Manifesto for Closing the Advantage Gap.* Carmarthen: Crown House Publishing Ltd.

Gladwell, M (2008) *Outliers: The Story of Success.* New York: Little, Brown.

Hambrick, D Z, Altmann, E M, Oswald, F L, Meinz, E J and Gobet, F (2007) Facing Facts About Deliberate Practice. *Psychological Perspectives on Expertise,* 5: 751.

Hirsch, E D Jr, Kett, J F and Trefil, J S (1988) *Cultural Literacy: What Every American Needs to Know.* New York: Vintage.

Levy, F and Murnane, R J (2012) *The New Division of Labor: How Computers Are Creating the Next Job Market.* Princeton, NJ: Princeton University Press.

Mccrea, P (2018) *Learning: What Is It, and How Might We Catalyse It?* London: Ambition Institute.

Tricot, A and Sweller, J (2014) Domain-Specific Knowledge and Why Teaching Generic Skills Does Not Work. *Educational Psychology Review,* 26: 265–83.

Weinstein, Y and Sumeracki, M (2018) *Understanding How We Learn: A Visual Guide*. London and New York: Routledge.

Willingham, D (2008a) What Will Improve a Student's Memory? *American Educator*, 32(4): 17-25.

Willingham, D (2008b) Learning Styles Don't Exist. YouTube. [online] Available at: www.youtube.com/watch?v=slv9rz2NTUk (accessed 15 February 2021).

Willingham, D (2010) *Why Don't Students Like School? A Cognitive Scientist Answers Questions About How the Mind Works and What It Means for the Classroom*. San Francisco, CA: Jossey-Bass.

4. ASSESSMENT AND TESTING

Key information

- Assessment and testing are the power tools of learning.
- Effective teaching uses assessment and testing to evaluate how students are doing, work out next steps, and adjust teaching accordingly.
- Feedback from assessment and testing is only effective if it is actually used by a learner.
- Grades represent more than just your child's achievement, so careful interpretation of them is needed.
- Assessment and testing themselves are neither good nor bad, but the ways in which they are administered, interpreted and used can be.

Do you have good memories of the assessments and tests you experienced when you were at school? For many people, the answer to this question will be a confident 'no'. It's common for assessment and testing – some of the 'power tools' of education – to be poorly understood and misused, and to be demotivating and anxiety-inducing. Understanding more about them – their uses and limitations – can help you to collaborate with your child's school.

We've already seen that, when learners engage in retrieval practice (often, using practice testing), they tend to learn more than similar learners who don't. But the power of testing is not limited solely to retrieval, and in this chapter we explore what assessment and testing actually are – and the benefits they can offer your child – by answering the following questions.

1. What is the difference between 'assessment' and 'testing'?
2. How do teachers use assessment and testing in the classroom?
3. Are marking and grades useful for my child's learning?
4. What tests do children have to take in primary and secondary school?

Question 1: What is the difference between 'assessment and testing'?

Assessment and testing are powerful tools for learning and any teacher or student can use them. But like any tool, they can be used skilfully (if you know what you're doing), or they can be used poorly (if you lack the required knowledge and skill). Once again, the Bananarama Principle in education returns; with assessment and testing in particular, however, it's both what you do and the way that you do it...

ASSESSMENT

Assessment is a process that has been described by Emeritus Professor of Educational Assessment at University College London, Dylan Wiliam, as '*the bridge between teaching and learning*'. Good assessment helps teachers and students clarify what they know and don't know, how they're getting on as they learn new material, and whether or not they have achieved the goals or standards set.

Ask the expert

In 2017 Evidence-Based Education, an organisation co-founded by Stuart Kime and Jack Deverson, brought together a panel of education experts at a primary school in London to answer the question 'What makes great assessment?' Here's what they said.

Professor Dame Alison Peacock (CEO of the Chartered College of Teaching): *Assessment, whether summative or formative, used as a tool to inform ongoing learning, is rigorous and supportive. The process of assessment should not be seen by the child or her teacher, as the end point, but as the beginning of future achievement.*

Tim Oates (Group Director of Assessment Research and Development at Cambridge Assessment): *Great assessment is accurate. It measures things with fidelity, and by doing this, provides valuable information.*

Daisy Christodoulou (Director of Education at No More Marking): *There are dozens of reasons why you might assess pupils, and the ideal type of assessment is different depending on the purpose. If you are assessing to find out what a pupil's predicted grade might be, that's very different from assessing to find out how you should adapt your next lesson given your pupils' strengths and weaknesses. An assessment that is perfect for working out a predicted grade might be terrible at identifying strengths and weaknesses. So until you are clear about exactly what your different purposes are, you won't be able to use the right assessments.*

Sarah Lee (former headteacher at Tarporley High School and Sixth Form): *Great assessment is great responsive teaching. Assessment is inextricable from teaching, and the quality of one is dependent on the quality of the other.*

Professor Rob Coe (Director of Research and Development at Evidence Based Education): *Assessment should tell you something new: often enough for it to be valuable, but not so often that it undermines your judgement. Assessment should inform judgement, not replace it; but equally, a single judgement is not an assessment.*

David Weston (CEO of the Teacher Development Trust): *Great assessment must be incredibly carefully designed. It needs to elicit information that can prompt helpful reflection by the pupil. It needs to reveal enough to the teacher to allow her to give useful feedback. It needs to relate to the curriculum 'map', strategically challenging pupils to recall and strengthen the right pieces of learning and understanding.*

Assessment is both vital and really hard to get right: remember that teachers are trying to pin down and understand something that is invisible. Learning can't be seen, so assessment processes help teachers to generate visible representations of it – children's answers to quiz questions, performances they give, demonstrations they do, and so on. The skill of great assessment lies in being able to find ways for children to show what they know and can do (sometimes in the form of tests), and to interpret the information they provide accurately and meaningfully. Ultimately, the goal of great assessment is to promote learning.

TESTS

If assessment is a process, then a test is an event during which a person produces responses to some kind of stimulus (like a question or an instruction) which, ideally, provide useful information and promote learning. A driving test, for example, generates information about road safety to the examiner, but also provides an opportunity for a driver to increase their knowledge and experience of road use. Similarly, a test in mathematics may help a teacher to identify gaps and misconceptions in a child's knowledge but the act of being tested also helps the child think hard about some element of mathematics.

While 'test' is a word that tends to have negative connotations for some in education, tests themselves are actually neither good nor bad. But the ways in which they are interpreted and used can be, so schools and colleges work hard to maximise the positive impact of them and reduce the adverse consequences.

Sometimes, a test in school will generate data (such as a score in the form of a percentage or letter grade) which are then interpreted by teachers, by students and by parents. It's at this stage of the assessment process that someone looking at the score *makes meaning* out of test data that has been generated: for one person, getting 75 per cent is interpreted as a big success, while for someone else, 75 per cent is considered a failure.

For example, a teacher who knows about the specific misconceptions and gaps in knowledge that a child in their class has might view 75 per cent as a triumph for that student. For someone not as familiar with the child and their current state of knowledge, that same percentage may be troubling. Careful and appropriate interpretation of test data by all who encounter and use it is a crucial step in making sure the information it contains is understood correctly. Close and constructive collaboration between teachers, parents and students is vital in this respect, so making use of every opportunity for open dialogue about grades and what they mean should be a priority.

Back in 1968, the American psychologist David Ausubel put the importance of assessment and testing as an integral aspect of education front-and-centre, by saying that the biggest factor influencing learning is what a child already knows. Teachers, he contended, should '*find out what this is and teach accordingly*' (Ausubel et al, 1968). Without assessment and testing, teachers can't do this.

Summary

Assessment is a process that goes on each and every day in school, and it's a process that's designed to make visible the important - but invisible - details of learning through the use of tests, quizzes, conversations, portfolios, demonstrations and a range of other techniques. In many ways, assessment is the very thing that enables your school's teachers to understand how your child is doing. Only then can they make informed decisions about what to do next to support progress.

Question 2: How do teachers use assessment and testing in the classroom?

Effective teachers evaluate how their students are doing, they reflect on what would best support them to move forward, and they adjust their teaching accordingly (often while it's happening in the dynamic environment of the classroom) (Wiliam, 2011).

During the course of a lesson or sequence of lessons, teachers take 'multiple inadequate glances' at how a child is doing, and build up a picture of students' learning using the 'power tools' of the assessment process such as moment-by-moment questioning, hinge questions at key moments in a teaching sequence (we'll look at these questions in detail later in the chapter), self-assessment and peer-assessment techniques.

By taking these 'multiple inadequate glances' through a variety of 'lenses' (using different types of testing), teachers can more confidently interpret the evidence of how a child is getting on. In essence, by seeking several different points of view on the same thing (for instance, the development of fluency in the use of algebra) and triangulating their interpretations, teachers reduce the chances of coming to an incorrect conclusion. They reduce them, but never eliminate them: learning is invisible, and assessing it is hard.

These 'multiple inadequate glances' form the bridge between teaching and learning, but research evidence also reveals that testing can benefit learners in even more ways than this.

In 2011, Professor Henry Roediger and a group of researchers in the United States summarised the evidence indicating the different ways testing can - directly and indirectly - support students' learning. Table 4A lists the ten benefits that they identified (Roediger et al, 2011).

Table 4A Ten benefits of testing

BENEFIT 1	The testing effect: retrieval aids later retention.
BENEFIT 2	Testing identifies gaps in knowledge.
BENEFIT 3	Testing causes students to learn more from the next learning episode.

$\longrightarrow$

Table 4A (Cont.)

BENEFIT 4	Testing produces better organisation of knowledge.
BENEFIT 5	Testing improves transfer of knowledge to new contexts.
BENEFIT 6	Testing can facilitate retrieval of information that was not tested.
BENEFIT 7	Testing improves metacognitive monitoring.
BENEFIT 8	Testing prevents interference from prior material when learning new material.
BENEFIT 9	Testing provides feedback to teachers.
BENEFIT 10	Frequent testing encourages students to study.

This is some list! Reading through it, it's helpful to keep in mind the caution given by the Bananarama Principle – testing 'used well' can provide these benefits. Testing used poorly or inappropriately won't.

Even when used well, such benefits can only be realised through the decisions and actions that teachers and their students take day in, day out. So how do teachers use the multiple inadequate glances taken through the lens of assessment and testing to guide teaching and support learning?

PRE-FLIGHT CHECKS

The act of teaching is a little like flying a plane (although arguably a lot more complex). A teacher – like a pilot – has a destination they are trying to help their students reach, and they have a route plotted to help them try and reach it (the curriculum, about which you'll read more in a later chapter). Prior to 'take-off' (before starting to teach their students) a good teacher will use assessment to find out what the children in their class know and don't know – doing so helps to set the course for the sequence of lessons to follow (teaching children what they already know is a redundant activity, and teaching them things for which they don't have sufficient prior knowledge is confusing and demotivating for all concerned).

Once the teacher and their students have done their 'pre-flight checks', it's time for take-off.

IN-FLIGHT CHECKS

After a pilot has a taken off and is en route to the planned destination, a series of checks is continually undertaken to ensure that the plane remains safely on course. In the face of changing wind speeds, fog and air traffic, pilots must constantly know not only where they're going, but how they're getting on (their heading and speed, for example), and what they need to do next in order to reach the destination.

Similarly, all manner of things can affect the 'course' of learning in a classroom, and assessment provides the 'in-flight checks' that a teacher uses to know if 'corrections' to the course are needed. But how often should they do this in the dynamic and rapidly changing environment of the classroom?

Former teacher and academic Dylan Wiliam has said that a teacher should not use assessment to promote learning in the classroom more than once every five seconds. He was trying to reinforce the point that this kind of assessment is ongoing, frequent and often almost imperceptible (perhaps even to the teacher doing it). In practice, there are lots of different ways in which a teacher can use assessment to promote learning, but one that is particularly powerful is the use of a 'hinge question' in the middle of a lesson (used to see if everyone in the classroom has secured a key piece of knowledge needed to move on to the next steps in the plan).

Hinge questions

One formulation of the 'in-flight' check that teachers use is known as the 'hinge question'. In his book, *Embedded Formative Assessment* (Wiliam, 2011), Wiliam talks about the power of questioning in lessons, recommending that lessons should be designed to include key points (the so-called 'hinges') at which learning is checked by asking questions to inform next-steps decisions. By using well-constructed hinge questions, a teacher is able to check if everyone in the room is ready to move on, and make evidence-informed decisions, not hope-filled assumptions.

Just as a pilot checks the course of a flight and adjusts it as needed, so the next phase of a lesson should be informed by the responses students give to the hinge question(s). Dylan suggests that there are two key considerations for teachers using these questions to help them work out what to do next.

1. The hinge question process should take no more than two minutes (ideally less than a minute) for all students to respond.
2. Teachers need to be able to see responses from every student within 15–20 seconds.

Ideally, the entire process of asking good questions, receiving answers and using them to determine what happens next in a lesson should be efficient and disrupt the flow of a lesson only minimally. Done well, it will seem almost imperceptible to most observers.

THE IMPORTANCE OF SURPRISE IN ASSESSMENT AND TESTING

Who among us likes to be told that we're wrong about something? Especially when it comes to a child in school, no parent or teacher relishes finding out that what they thought previously was, in fact, incorrect.

Assessment and testing done well will always confront teachers, parents and children with this unwanted surprise. Taking multiple inadequate glances tends to throw up pieces of information that don't always align or agree with each other, and this complexity can be harder to deal with (both cognitively and emotionally). Yet remaining open to surprise is the only way that we can make truly effective use of assessment and testing.

The fact that the pieces of information we gather about learning from the assessment process don't agree can – counterintuitively – be helpful. So long as we're able to cope with the task of combining the pieces, the result is more likely to be a more dependable and more realistic representation of what a child knows and can do.

As a mindset, it's helpful to think of being surprised as a desirable goal of assessment and testing, because it means you are open to updating your understanding about a child's learning. Of course, most of us don't really like anything that tells us we might have been wrong about something, so developing this mindset requires a conscious effort for most of us, and a constructive, open dialogue with teachers and leaders.

FEEDBACK

Another way in which teachers use the information from assessment and testing to promote learning is with the addition of feedback (information regarding an aspect of a child's performance on a specific task (Kluger and DeNisi, 1996) which generally has the eventual aim of improving learning, either directly or indirectly (Shute, 2008)). Broadly speaking, there are two key types of feedback.

- **Performance evaluation:** this often comes in the form of a grade on a piece of work or an overall comment that indicates to a learner whether they are working at the desired level.
- **Guidance and advice:** this often comes in the form of an ongoing dialogue between students and teachers. It indicates how a learner is getting on and what they can do next to work towards their goal.

Written marking on students' assignments is one of the most familiar modes of feedback, despite the fact that there is little research evidence which supports its continued use (something we'll explore later in this chapter). Feedback comes in a vast array of forms, and the art of a great classroom teacher is to fit the type of feedback they use to the task in hand and the student undertaking it.

When, for example, your child responds to a hinge question during a lesson and the teacher says, '*Yes, that's the correct answer*', that is a form of feedback. When handing back homework and the teacher says '*Great work*', that is a form of feedback. Circling a student's response is a form of feedback. Even smiling and nodding during a presentation is a subtle form of feedback. Taken together, all this constant feedback *can* have an effect on student learning, but the skill of a great teacher is to ensure that this effect is a positive one.

Not all feedback has a positive effect (saying '*well done*' may make a child feel better about themselves for a short period, but rarely does it help them make progress due to the lack of specific next steps they could take). Even when the feedback is designed and given well, it can only ever be effective if it's actually used by a learner. Skilled teachers break down complex tasks, identify where the child has weak links, and provide feedback that helps to reinforce knowledge. Irrespective of which type of feedback your child receives, there are two key ingredients that are likely to make it effective.

1. **High-quality information** from the feedback provider (for example, the teacher, or another student).
2. **Communication** of this information to – and **use** of it by – the child.

Adding feedback into assessment and testing can really make a difference to learning, but only if it contains something important for the learner, is understood by them, and is used. Feedback is a learner's possession, and only they can realise its value.

If assessment is a process, then tests are the tools used by teachers and students within it. Testing often gets a bad name, but research evidence indicates that it has huge potential to help children learn, often by creating the circumstances where they have to think hard about something and use what they know to generate an answer. Critically, testing provides the raw information that teachers interpret and use as the basis for another of learning's powerful tools: feedback.

Question 3: Are marking and grades useful for my child's learning?

MARKING

One of the ways in which feedback is communicated to students is through a process of marking. Marking can be defined as the provision of written marks and feedback comments (and sometimes grades) on children's work by others (generally teachers) and is a common practice that is often connected to assessment and testing. It's one that most of us who went to school in England will be familiar with. 'Could do better'; 'You have problems with organisation. Please sort them'; 'Excellent work' and other hollow phrases have littered the pages of children's books for years, and kept the makers of red pens in healthy business.

Despite the fact that marking is still a very common practice in many schools (even, bizarrely, for children who are not yet able to read the words put on their work), there is very little research evidence to indicate whether or not it's useful in helping students learn. Schools do lots of it, but there is little or no robust justification for it. It's mostly a waste of time, energy and ink.

Ofsted, the schools' regulator, is clear on what it expects and does not expect when it comes to marking:

Ofsted recognises that marking and feedback to pupils, both written and oral, are important aspects of assessment. However, Ofsted does not expect to see any specific frequency, type or volume of marking and feedback; these are for the school to decide through its assessment policy. Marking and feedback should be consistent with that policy, which may cater for different subjects and different age groups of pupils in different ways, in order to be effective and efficient in promoting learning.

(Ofsted, 2018, p 13)

Pause for a moment to think about the experience of a secondary school English teacher marking a set of books and giving written feedback on each. Imagine that the teacher spends 10–15 minutes reading through each child's writing task, and then spends another five minutes writing a comment on them. Now multiply the time taken by the number of children in the class (30, for instance). With 30 children, the whole process could take around ten hours, and when you add in other classes that the teacher may teach, you start to get to some very long hours indeed.

It's up to your child's school to make decisions about the use of marking and feedback and ensure that these are implemented according to the policy decisions they make. While marking books and putting detailed written feedback comments in them may give the appearance of good teaching, it's a poor indicator of the quality of education your child is receiving, so be sceptical about what its presence or absence tells you. Ask your child what they actually do when they get their book back from the teacher. Do they read the comments that took so long to write? Do they act on them? Do they know more as a result? The most important thing about any form of feedback is what a child does with it and, increasingly, many teachers and school leaders are debating the effectiveness and efficiency of written marking, especially as technology has created new possibilities for the delivery of it.

But written comments are not the only thing that most parents will associated with the word 'feedback'. Alongside words in the margin or a sentence/paragraph at the end of an assignment, teachers sometimes provide a grade as a form of evaluative feedback. As you might expect, the use of grades is another topic of some contention, and worth looking at in some detail.

GRADES

Grades are a form of shorthand used by schools to communicate a lot of information quickly. In the nineteenth century, they were sometimes presented orally by a teacher during a visit to the child's home, a practice that was replaced during the twentieth century due to the increasing numbers of students and subjects they studied. With time and resources increasingly at a premium, schools tried to find ways that would enable them to continue communicating with parents and others, but in a more efficient manner; percentages began to become part of this communication, something which arguably reduced – rather than enhanced – the understanding of what a child knew or could do. Written reports at the end of the school term or year became the norm.

Nowadays, you don't have a personal home visit from your child's teacher to communicate and explain their grades (although many schools have parents' evenings), and without a skilled teacher discussing what they mean and how to interpret them correctly, grades themselves – mere letters or numbers – have to work very hard indeed to convey all the meaning that is hidden within them.

Think, for instance, of your child arriving home with a grade for a piece of work on life during the Iron Age – they got a grade 6. What does grade 6 mean to you? In what ways is it better than a 5, and not as good as a 7? On its own, the individual grade is a very limited piece of information (if, indeed, you can interpret correctly the information it holds!). Moreover, to what extent does that grade 6 act only as a measure of achievement? Were other things contributing to it that remain unseen or unexplained?

When you're reviewing your child's grades it's easy to think that what you're looking at is a measure of pure achievement, but this is rarely the case, according to researchers who have reviewed a century's worth of studies into grading (Brookhart et al, 2016).

LOOKING BEHIND THE GRADE

Teachers – like all humans – find purely objective judgements (like the assignment of a single grade to represent the quality of a piece of work) both desirable and impossible to make. So, when it comes to grading, you shouldn't be surprised that the grade assigned – either to a single piece of work or as a summary grade on a report card – represents more than just your child's achievement in a subject. Researcher Susan Brookhart and her co-authors identified several factors that are also likely to affect your child's grade (other than their achievement):

- behaviour;
- effort;
- persistence;
- perceived ability;
- participation.

A grade is a representation of more than just achievement. And, while it is tempting to want to improve this shorthand so common in schools, to make it more objective, we have to remember that teachers are busy human beings who are trying to convey as best they can a summary of some really complex information in a single letter or number. It's hard to achieve precision, and important to acknowledge that a whole range of different things that teachers and leaders value get mixed in together in most grading processes. Consequently, it is important to use every opportunity you have to speak directly with your child's teachers to understand all of the information behind the grade.

WHEN CAN GRADES BE USEFUL?

Grades can be both useful and highly relevant to children at key points in their education such as in the months leading up to Key Stage 4 GCSE exams: knowing how you're doing in relation to the level you're trying to achieve can be really helpful. At other points, however, grades can have a detrimental effect: they can demotivate the motivated; they can convince the overconfident that they don't need to work any harder. Ultimately, their use is a judgement call for teachers and leaders, but one that should be informed by the best available evidence on their likely effects for students' learning.

Summary

Marking and grades try to represent lots of detailed information, but can lose the details that were originally thought about when the teacher assigned them to your child's work, so don't over-interpret them or read too much into them, and talk to your child's teachers if you have questions about them. Also, remember that a grade is rarely just a measure of pure achievement, and a conversation with your child's teacher about all the other things that are behind the letter or number might be really informative for you.

Question 4: What tests do children have to take in primary and secondary school?

National, statutory tests such as those in Key Stage 2 (often called 'SATs') and GCSEs at the end of Key Stage 4 attract lots of (often unwelcome) attention each year (especially during the massive upheaval of statutory testing brought about by the COVID-19 pandemic), and more than they really deserve. A disproportionate amount of time and attention focused on them can translate into mounting stresses for students, parents, and teachers and school leaders. While these tests can be helpful to children in lots of ways, how they are hyped up, reported (especially in the notoriously 'quiet news' period of August when GCSE and A level results are published) and interpreted often has quite the opposite effect.

Some critics of testing have claimed that children in England are among the most highly tested in the world, but this is not true. While there is definitely a sense of importance that comes from the part played by test results in the accountability of schools, Hong Kong and Singapore's high-performing education systems, for example, test their primary school children far more than English schools test theirs.

At the heart of this heated testing debate is stress (a topic we'll explore in greater depth in Chapter 8), especially when it comes to the Key Stage 2 tests in Year 6 or GCSEs in Year 11, for example. Alongside this sits the worry that time taken up with testing is time taken away

WHAT EVERY PARENT SHOULD KNOW ABOUT EDUCATION

from teaching. There is pressure for schools to perform well, and this pressure has often been transferred, unintentionally, from the school to the children who attend it. Yet it is not the tests themselves that are at fault, but the way many school leaders, teachers, parents and children have become accustomed to preparing for them (by virtue of wanting to help learners perform to the very highest level possible), the way some in the media talk about them, and the inappropriately high status given to the results. Tests are not bad, per se, but they can be used in ways that are not conducive to either learning or good mental health.

One way in which you can collaborate with your child's school to support their learning is to know which statutory tests your child will take, why they take them, and what they can (and can't) tell you. Below, we've outlined the main statutory tests in England.

YEAR 1 PHONICS CHECK

In June of the school year, children in Year 1 of primary school read 40 words aloud to their teacher in this test of phonological awareness (the ability to differentiate the individual sounds which make up spoken words). While a lot of parents feel anxious about these tests, research evidence has established a clear link between poor phonological awareness and later literacy development. So, it's worth knowing if your child needs extra support in this area (if a child doesn't meet the standards set by the government, they have to take the test again in Year 2).

As your child gets older and moves through school, they will encounter the further series of tests. We've given an outline of these in Table 4B.

Table 4B Key Stage 1-4 statutory test areas

KEY STAGE 1	Key Stage 1 tests happen in May for children in Year 2 and are aimed at knowing what children can do in the following areas: - English reading - English grammar, punctuation and spelling - Maths Your school should let you know how your child has done in these tests by the end of the summer term.
KEY STAGE 2	Key Stage 2 tests happen in May for children in Year 6 and are aimed at establishing how well children are doing in the following areas: - English reading - English grammar, punctuation and spelling - Maths
KEY STAGE 3	There are no statutory tests at the end of Key Stage 3 (Year 9).

Table 4B (Cont.)

KEY STAGE 4	At the end of Key Stage 4, most children take GCSE exams in the following compulsory subjects: • English • Maths • Science Children will also be examined in the optional subjects they have studied, such as: • Arts • Design and technology • Humanities • Modern foreign languages Achievement in GCSE is represented with a number from 9 (the highest grade achievable) to 1 (the lowest grade achievable).

Statutory testing gives a valuable insight into how children are progressing in certain key areas, and the results achieved at Key Stage 4 provide a form of 'currency' that young people use to move on to employment and further study. Their importance shouldn't be understated, and nor should the potential for anxiety and stress that can come from inflating their role in the process of a child's education. But as we mentioned earlier on, the Bananarama Principle reminds us that it's not tests themselves that cause the problem, but the way that they're viewed, used and talked about in our education systems.

Summary

Statutory testing is actually a relatively small part of the assessment processes that your child will experience during their time in school. Many of these attract a lot of attention both in school (from teachers and leaders, for instance) and out (from the media and politicians), so it's important to acknowledge the unintended consequences for your child and others of raising their stakes: statutory testing is not, itself, detrimental to children, but the ways in which we talk about it and use the results from it can be.

❖ What to talk about at parents' evening

From a teacher's perspective, *assessment* and *testing* are words that can still conjure up negative connotations for a variety of reasons. Exam grades have been used by some schools as the basis for performance-related pay decisions, and significant workload has been created for many teachers as a result of some of the administrative tasks associated with testing (marking and uploading data, for instance). So, while talking to your child's teacher about how they use assessment to support your child's learning is a really important thing, be mindful that it can be an emotive topic.

When you have the opportunity to speak to your child's teachers at a parent–teacher meeting, here are three things about assessment and testing worth discussing.

- **Assessment to support learning.** How do assessment, testing and feedback combine to support my child to learn?

- **Find out what is behind the grade.** Teachers have a deep understanding of how your child is doing, so consider asking: What's *behind a grade* or a comment? Remember that grades are not precise, so don't depend on them too heavily – the conversation about how your child manages themselves during lessons and what they need to improve or work on next is far more useful to you and your child.

- **Stress and anxiety.** In Chapter 8 we look in more depth at mental health and stress, but you could ask how teachers limit and manage anxiety and stress from assessment and testing. Remember the Bananarama Principle and find out what the school already does to help your child approach assessment and testing as a positive aspect of school, and how they manage the potential negative impacts.

Conclusion

Above all else, assessment and testing used in your child's school should align with and focus on the curriculum – the things that your school has set out as the educational entitlement designed to help your child develop and realise their fullest potential.

further reading

If you want to find out more about assessment, you can find an interesting series of freely available ebooks at https://evidence-based-education.thinkific.com/courses/resource-library. The following books may also be of interest:

» Paul Black and Dylan Wiliam's *Inside the Black Box: Raising Standards through Classroom Assessment* (2005) is one of the seminal books on assessment in the classroom (and it's only 21 pages long!).

> » Daniel Willingham's book *Why Don't Students Like School? A Cognitive Scientist Answers Questions About How the Mind Works and What It Means for the Classroom* (2010) is a great read, and gives an insight into key findings about learning from cognitive science research.

Bibliography

Ausubel, D P, Novak, J D and Hanesian, H (1968) *Educational Psychology: A Cognitive View*. New York: Holt, Rinehart and Winston.

Black, P and Wiliam, D (2005) *Inside the Black Box: Raising Standards Through Classroom Assessment*. London: Granada Learning.

Brookhart, S M, Guskey, T R, Bowers, A J, McMillan, J H, Smith, J K, Smith, L F, Stevens, M T and Welsh, M E (2016) A Century of Grading Research: Meaning and Value in the Most Common Educational Measure. *Review of Educational Research*, 86(4): 803–48.

Kluger, A N and DeNisi, A (1996) The Effects of Feedback Interventions on Performance: A Historical Review, a Meta-Analysis, and a Preliminary Feedback Intervention Theory. *Psychological Bulletin*, 119(2): 254.

Ofsted (2018) *School Inspection Handbook (No. 150066)*. London: Ofsted.

Roediger, H L III, Putnam, A L and Smith, M A (2011) Ten Benefits of Testing and Their Applications to Educational Practice. *Psychology of Learning* and *Motivation*, 55: 1–36.

Shute, V J (2008) Focus on Formative Feedback. *Review of Educational Research*, 78(1): 153–89.

Wiliam, D (2011) *Embedded Formative Assessment*. Bloomington, IN: Solution Tree Press.

Willingham, D (2010) *Why Don't Students Like School? A Cognitive Scientist Answers Questions About How the Mind Works and What It Means for the Classroom*. San Francisco, CA: Jossey-Bass.

5. PUTTING IT INTO PRACTICE IN THE CLASSROOM AND AT HOME

Time to reflect

In the last couple of chapters you have discovered that:

- learning is a complex, long-term process that requires regular reinforcement which cannot easily be captured by tests and exams;
- learning must be revisited and strengthened in order to transfer knowledge from working memory into long-term memory and construct the effective mental models that a child requires to have 'learnt' something;
- in the classroom, good assessment is primarily used a tool for helping with this learning process, not for evaluating the intelligence or effort of students.

This chapter provides the kinds of learning strategies that put these ideas into practice in the home environment. This is where we put education research into practice. These should not be understood as using the 'correct' strategies, as individual circumstances and implementation can drastically impact on their effectiveness. However, each one represents a 'best bet' approach for which there is considerable evidence of its efficacy. These also represent the kinds of strategies that research-informed teachers may well be using in the classroom.

The strategies explored in this chapter

1. Test yourself to commit knowledge to memory
2. Revisit learning at regular intervals
3. Manage difficulty and effort to maximise learning
4. Use worked examples and model answers
5. Connect knowledge together to deepen understanding
6. Present information visually to strengthen memory

Strategy 1: Test yourself to commit knowledge to memory

One massively important stage in the learning process is to transfer knowledge from working memory to long-term memory. The main strategy to achieve this is the process that psychologists call **retrieval practice**. This means repeatedly retrieving knowledge from long-term memory into working memory and using it. This serves two purposes. First, it causes the brain to strengthen the storage of that memory for future use. Second, it makes the content of the memory visible for the student (and the teacher) to correct and improve.

HOW MIGHT A TEACHER USE THIS STRATEGY?

Teachers using retrieval practice effectively tend to focus on making the exact knowledge students are required to learn clear and visible, as well as providing resources to help them learn and regularly requiring them to remember the key information in class. This may include:

- giving children quizzes on key knowledge;
- maintaining a culture of questioning and remembering in the classroom, constantly getting students to recall and think about existing knowledge;
- setting homework that requires students to learn specific information;
- creating memory resources for children such as knowledge organisers (quick summary sheets of key knowledge) and getting them to quiz themselves on them;
- getting children to revisit learning at the beginning and end of lessons through recap tasks or short quizzes.

HOW A STUDENT MIGHT USE THIS STRATEGY

Students are increasingly encouraged to make retrieval practice part of their regular learning habits. Effective learners will regularly self-quiz, particularly as they reach the end of secondary school.

- Self-quizzing from notes, flashcards or learning resources provided by teachers. Please note, there are now a large number of high-quality digital flashcard and memorisation tools available to students for free. The most famous are services like Quizlet (www.quizlet.com) and StudyStack (www.studystack.com).
- Writing summary notes after a lesson – the note-taking system outlined later in this chapter is particularly good, as it forces students to review and learn their notes.

HOW YOU CAN HELP WITH THIS

You can help encourage a culture of retrieval practice by:

- showing enthusiasm for retrieval practice, helping children to make a game of it and integrate it into their homework routines;
- taking part in retrieval practice with children, acting as 'quizmaster' or even learning along with them;
- building retrieval practice into everyday experiences – parents tend to do this naturally when children are very young (asking your child to name animals at the zoo, for example), but there is no reason this shouldn't continue and develop as the child gets older;
- going through a child's lesson with them and getting them to tell you the key information then helping them to write it down in the form of summary notes.

Strategy 2: Revisit learning at regular intervals

One of the most obvious truths about memory is that it fades over time. Research has shown that spacing out retrieval practice has a powerful effect on memory. We can harness what the psychologists Elizabeth and Robert Bjork have called '*the power of forgetting*'; the deeper we have to dig to retrieve knowledge from long-term memory, the more powerful the memory becomes.

HOW A TEACHER MIGHT USE THIS STRATEGY

Effective teachers make sure students revisit topics regularly, but with appropriate gaps between learning incidents. This may include:

- moving from a purely topic-based plan for lessons, to a plan that focuses on learning, regularly revisiting topics at intervals to deepen memory and understanding (interleaving);
- planning assessments that revisit learning at regularly spaced intervals such as recap quizzes, knowledge reviews (where students self-rate their understanding of key knowledge) and practice questions.

HOW A STUDENT MIGHT USE THIS STRATEGY

When studying by themselves, students need to be aware that spacing their learning out is superior to doing it in one go and:

- plan gaps between studying topics;
- consciously wait between studying a topic and testing themselves on it;
- revisit older topics on a regular basis;
- when revising, cycle through topics on a regular basis.

HOW YOU MIGHT HELP WITH THIS STRATEGY

- Encourage your child to deliberately space learning.
- Help them to plan a revision structure.
- Ask questions about older topics.

Strategy 3: Manage difficulty and effort to maximise learning

In Chapter 3 you learned about **cognitive load theory**, the idea that students have finite cognitive capacity in working memory, but endless space in their long-term memory. We also discussed the related idea of **desirable difficulty**; that learning must inherently be challenging to be effective. Taken together, the two ideas mean that teachers have to make sure that they are managing the cognitive effort required and minimise distractions so as to prevent cognitive overload, while also keep students in that 'sweet spot' of effective difficulty.

HOW A TEACHER MIGHT USE THIS

Effective teachers manage cognitive load by:

- using scaffolds and worked examples (solved equations or model essays, for example), but slowly removing them as students gain mastery of the topic or skill;
- minimising distraction in the classroom;
- removing excessive information and visual noise from presentations, handout and explanations;
- repeatedly emphasising and reinforcing key information during the lesson, providing multiple opportunities to revisit and repeat that key information over the course of the lesson and beyond.

HOW A STUDENT MIGHT USE THIS

Students need to be aware that failure on a task doesn't necessarily indicate insufficient effort and seeking to build your knowledge on a topic may be more effective than just trying again harder. Build up steadily but challenge yourself on a regular basis to make sure you are maximising your learning potential.

- Explore model answers or worked examples to gain a sense of quality and to set your sights.
- Identify the things you struggled with and study and practise them in isolation before trying the task again.
- Strip away distractions while studying. Music or access to a mobile phone can completely undermine attention to the task at hand.

HOW YOU MIGHT HELP WITH THIS

Parents should try to create an effective environment for learning at home.

- Decouple effort from achievement, which means praising when your child is working hard to complete a challenging task, irrespective of their success.
- Learn to recognise when your child needs additional help to achieve success on a task, but praise their effort. Equally, don't be afraid to let them work hard to find a solution if you think it should be within their grasp. In most cases, you shouldn't seek to reduce cognitive load completely (ie, completing the task for them) but slowing increasing the scaffolding necessary

WHAT EVERY PARENT SHOULD KNOW ABOUT EDUCATION

to complete the task until they are just about able to do it for themselves. Offering no support means the child will continue to fail; solving the task for them will reduce all cognitive load completely and thus minimise learning. You want them to have to work hard, even struggle, but not to the point of disappointment and failure.

Putting it into practice

How to support a child with their homework without making it too easy for them:

1. **Do I know enough?** It can be a dangerous assumption that you as an adult automatically know the topic well enough to help. Check the students' notes, or search information online. Identify key terms and questions that are at the heart of the topic.

2. **Stimulate their memory.** Challenge and prompt them to remember the key information they learnt in class, especially the key terms, concepts and structures the teacher has suggested they use. What you are hoping is that through an initial prompt they can make the connection to a solution or inspiration by themselves.

3. **Look at examples.** Has the child been given a model answer to look at? If not, ask the teacher if they have one available or look online to see if any are available (see recommendations in Strategy 4 below). Highlight effective vocabulary and language and talk to them about what makes them good. Encourage them to express their thoughts on the techniques and structures. There are some great books available (see the list at the end of the chapter) that have learnable essay-writing structures for children to use.

4. **Scaffold the task.** Walk through the essay-writing process with them, getting them to do as much of it as is possible. Emphasise the key stages as you do them together, getting the child to explain them back to you in order to check they understand.

Strategy 4: Use worked examples and model answers

A useful technique for scaffolding knowledge for a child is to get them to explore worked examples of the assessments they are required to complete. A worked example is just a finished version of a question; for example, a completed maths problem or a finished essay. This is an effective tool because it lightens the cognitive load for students who need it, while allowing them to see how success has been achieved. Looking at worked examples can help build a set of examples in the memory to draw upon when presented with a novel problem, as well as making the process of finding a solution visible to them.

HOW A TEACHER MIGHT USE THIS

Teachers should regularly introduce worked examples and get students to engage with them in a variety of ways.

- Narrating through the worked example, explaining what is effective about them and the thought processes required to complete them.
- Using a worked example as feedback, then getting students to revisit their original answer.
- Giving a worked example with parts missing and asking students to explain the missing parts.
- Getting students to analyse and summarise what they have learnt from looking at the model answer.

HOW A STUDENT MIGHT USE THIS

When studying by themselves, students can still use worked examples if provided by a teacher or obtained elsewhere. Study guides and textbooks often contain useful worked examples and students can make use of them effectively by:

- using them to compare and review their own responses;
- using them to help plan their own response;
- analysing them for techniques and methods.

HOW YOU MIGHT HELP WITH THIS

Parents can often help find high-quality worked examples that can help students understand things better. Good places to look are as follows.

- **Commercially available study guides.** Most high street and online bookstores have large sections that provide questions and solutions across a wide range of subjects. Those published by the exam boards themselves (AQA, OCR, Pearson, Edexcel) are often the best as they target the curriculum and use exam specialists. Similarly, trustworthy brands like Collins, CGP and the BBC publish high-quality resources.
- **Show them professional music, dance and theatre.** For students struggling with art-based subjects, engaging them with experiences and appreciation of professional-quality performances can be both instructional and inspirational.
- **Professional writing.** Students struggling with writing tasks may benefit from reading through high-quality writing of a similar genre with you. Has your child every read an article in a broadsheet newspaper or a high-quality periodical?
- **Online study services.** There are thousands of online study websites for skills such as maths, grammar and writing. Some are commercial, some are free. These can often provide rich veins of worked examples for students to explore and practise with.

Strategy 5: Connect knowledge together to deepen understanding

Once they have grasped the basic information, children deepen their understanding of a subject through connecting the knowledge together and repeatedly using it to think and solve problems in the subject. Revision isn't just flashcards; it is the application of the knowledge to achieve understanding and fluency. This is often a neglected part of the learning process, and parents and students alike can misinterpret the cognitive model of learning as 'do lots of quizzing', when quizzing itself is just one part of the process. Build upon prior knowledge to build better understanding.

HOW A TEACHER MIGHT USE THIS

Effective teachers embed this process at the heart of their practice, regularly challenging students to deepen their understanding and link knowledge to existing knowledge. Some ways they can do this are as follows.

- Asking connective questions: *How does A link to B? What other things we have learnt that A reminds you of?*
- Get students to reflect upon their understanding of concepts and ask questions.
- Get students to explain concepts to their partners.
- Highlighting and teaching links between topics.
- Revisiting a previous concept once the children have studied other related concepts.
- Introducing more challenging assessments as their understanding deepens.

HOW A STUDENT MIGHT USE THIS

Techniques students might use include:

- knowledge mapping, which means revisiting topics at the end of study and mapping them out as a mind map or similar. For example, if studying a novel, the map could be of all the key characters and the relationships between them.
- devising their own assessments on the information. This helps the student to think more deeply about the topic and how experts understand it.
- teaching the topic to someone else.

HOW YOU MIGHT HELP WITH THIS

Parents can have a very useful role in helping children to deepen their understanding, particularly with younger learners. Useful techniques involve:

- asking connective questions that encourage children to connect what they have learnt to other things they know: *How does this link to the topic you're studying? Have you seen anything like this before? What is the most important thing you've learnt in this topic?*
- getting children to explain concepts back to them, and then asking follow-up questions that get them to think deeper about what they are studying.

Strategy 6: Present information visually to strengthen memory

One of the most useful strategies for squeezing maximum learning out of a study session is a technique known as **dual coding**. This is a strategy whereby learners interact with or create visualisations of the things they are learning in order to reinforce memory. The science behind this approach is actually quite simple. We all have two different systems in our brain when we process information and store it, one verbal and one visual. When we learn something, if we engage with the information both verbally *and* visually then we get what is in effect a 'double lock' on that information because it is stored in both systems. In addition, while language is sequential (one word at a time) our memory isn't, and so while many of the ways we encounter knowledge are linguistic (books, lectures, etc) and therefore sequential, it helps a student's memory to be able to see the underlying information presented in a visual way. So rather than just hearing someone lecture you about themes of a book, seeing them mapped out in a visual diagram makes it easier to both understand them and store them in memory.

HOW A TEACHER MIGHT USE THIS STRATEGY

In class, a teacher may think about a suitable image or visualisation of the information they are presenting. If they are teaching the Tudor era, they may keep referring back to a timeline of the era to visualise the events they are otherwise presenting verbally. Similarly, they may draw an image on a board to summarise and reinforce a concept they have just explained. In lessons, they may ask students to complete tasks that take orally presented information (such as a scientific law) and ask them to create a visual representation to lock it in memory better.

HOW STUDENTS SHOULD USE THIS

Many students will already have a propensity for drawing that can easily be co-opted into improving their memory and understanding. Students should learn to use drawings and visualisations as part of note-taking, and learn the habit of backing up written learning with visualisations. For example: if a student is revising *Romeo and Juliet* for an exam, rather than just reviewing their notes on the main characters and events, they could instead choose to map out the major characters and events in the play, with small drawings of characters, scenes and locations to organise and maximise their memory.

Putting it into practice

WHAT DOES EFFECTIVE NOTE-TAKING LOOK LIKE?

If a child is successful in their GCSEs and A levels, the learning skill that is most crucial to their success is probably making and learning from notes. However, it's probably mislabelling to call this skill 'note-taking'. Just writing down things a teacher says is not note-taking in any meaningful sense, it's just the start of a process by which the experience of a lesson is turned into learning.

The primary purpose of any note-taking system is not to have a record of the lesson, but to help students in their longer-term goal task of learning knowledge. Any system that fails to focus on this long-term goal can be worse than not taking notes at all, as the act of taking notes can itself be a distraction (Carter and Van Matre, 1975). Unless there is a subsequent process to turn in-class notes into learning, they can be a waste of attention and effort. Most effective note-taking processes tend to have three stages.

1. **Capturing the information from the lesson.** This isn't as simple as it sounds as teachers don't always make it clear what is the most relevant information and students often lack the expertise to know exactly what is most important. Getting the right level of detail in your notes is a skill that requires practice and guidance from a teacher.

2. **Summarising the key information.** Once the raw lesson notes have been captured, the next stage is to revisit the information learnt in the lesson at home and try to condense it into effective summary notes that distil down to the most important essence.

3. **Learning the notes.** Committing the notes to memory and then developing a deep understanding of the concept through quizzing and questions.

HOW DO THE BEST TEACHERS APPROACH NOTE-TAKING?

Effective teachers direct note-taking during their lessons, making it clear what information is worth writing down and directing students to the best way to capture it. They will talk explicitly about the note-taking process, and share examples of good notes, or high-quality notes of their own. They tend to also have high expectations of the quality of students' notes and regularly check them. They may also provide their own notes if they believe it is a clearer and more efficient use of class time to do so, or that it might speed the knowledge acquisition process.

HOW YOUNG IS TOO YOUNG TO BE TAKING NOTES?

Note-taking is a difficult skill and one you would associate with higher qualifications like GCSEs and A levels, but even then, it would be a mistake to presume students arrive at those exams with their note-taking skills fully formed. At younger ages, children lack the learning experience and subject knowledge to note-take with efficiency. This is not to say that students shouldn't start to learn how do it, but that teachers may well lean more heavily on directly giving out notes or learning in class.

DO STUDENTS NEED TO TAKE NOTES IN THE DIGITAL AGE? ISN'T THAT A BIT OLD FASHIONED?

One common argument against traditional note-taking is the idea that in the current era handwritten notes are old-fashioned and inefficient. Certainly, it is true that in an age of photocopiers, digital learning environments and PowerPoint, the traditional model of the oral lecture with students taking written notes has been challenged. It is perfectly acceptable if a teacher wants to share their own summary notes with students. But is there still a value to traditional note-taking? The available evidence suggests that note-taking is a useful part of the wider learning process, and given that this remains the primary mode of study in university and a useful skill for the world of work, it remains an invaluable skill.

Ask a teacher

Dawn Cox is a teacher and blogger (https://missdcoxblog.wordpress.com/). She tweets under the handle @missdcox. She is the head of RE at Manningtree High School, Lawford.

How has learning about educational research changed the way you teach?

Overall, it has encouraged me to do more of the things I was already doing. For years, I have used quick quizzes at the start of lessons. However, having found out from research how important it is to help stop forgetting, it is now the start of the majority of my lessons. In fact, reflecting on last year, I spent about a third of most lessons on some sort of retrieval practice.

Another example is that I have always given students lists of keywords to learn but now I regularly test them on them. Not only does this make sure that they learn them, but the retrieval practice helps their long-term memory of the definitions.

It has also given me confidence to continue the way I have always taught, safe in the knowledge that it is supported by research, rather than having to try and 'hoop jump' through what someone else says makes a good lesson. I am lucky that my current school doesn't do this but, in the past, I was told things about learning that weren't research-based and I really struggled to see how I could do them with impact.

WHAT EVERY PARENT SHOULD KNOW ABOUT EDUCATION

What common teaching methods do you think are overrated or ineffective?

I'm not effective at teaching in groups. Maybe it is how I do it, but I can't see the benefit of using the time in this way, in my own teaching. I admire those that can get this to be time-effective and efficient for learning. I also do not waste time on things that might be considered 'fun' ways of presenting ideas unless I can see that the use of the method will have a significant impact on learning.

You've written on your blog that teachers should 'ditch revision'. What do you mean by this and how would it work in practice?

First, it links to the traditional idea of revision, which is a time, at the very end of a course, to go over previously taught material. This seems completely illogical if we focus on the real learning the first time it is taught. The only time we need to 're-teach' something is when a student doesn't understand and that should be as soon as they don't understand it, not at the end of the course. So, we should ditch the idea that any sort of intervention in terms of understanding should be left until the end. We should be supporting students every lesson and using any in-class intervention straight away. From this we need to think carefully about our curriculum, what we teach and when we teach it. If we aren't designing our curriculum for long-term learning, then what are we designing it for? I can use about a third of a lesson on retrieval. We therefore need to think carefully about how we structure and teach our curriculum to ensure it is all covered in time but is about learning, not just content coverage. I also think that we need to start the repetition of the work from lesson 2, to stop students from forgetting. Leaving it to a few months before the exams works (massed practice), but not as well as spaced practice from the moment of learning something. So, we should also ditch the idea that repetition and recall of content happens at the end of the course. If we spend more time on ensuring our lessons and the learning from them is good, it will stop the nonsense of after-school revision and staff giving up their holidays to revise with students.

In your classroom, how do you use assessments and tests to help students learn?

As mentioned, every lesson has some form of retrieval. This could be called a test. It will be a quick 1–10 of prior content, mixed up from a long time ago, more recent and from last lesson. I can see this has real impact on students' long-term memory of key concepts. They also tell me that these quick quizzes really help them make progress.

How do you make sure students transfer their knowledge from quizzing into deeper understanding?

If they know the meaning of subject specific vocabulary, they can use this confidently in their answers. They can also ensure that they are applying the correct knowledge to their answers.

I can 'see' the impact of this when students answer questions and ask questions in class. They wouldn't be able to ask certain things if the knowledge hadn't been embedded in their long-term memory. They can also make links between topics that shows me that they haven't just learnt these things in isolation but can synthesise them.

What does 'interleaving' mean in practice for you?

To me it simply means that students encounter subject knowledge more than once, at different times in the course. In a formal way, our GCSE schemes aren't taught in a linear fashion, following through sections of the GCSE where there may or may not be opportunities to make links. We mix up the sections, so they are forced to recall prior learning to access the next part of the curriculum. It is carefully planned. Informally, it means always linking new material to previously learnt content. This means they can make links, and this helps with their understanding and long-term memory.

Conclusion

There is no single correct way to learn, nor are there quick fixes that allow a student to circumvent the learning process. However, given the challenge learning presents, it makes sense to pick strategies that evidence indicates make learning as effective as possible. In this chapter we have condensed the most important strategies for effective learning and suggested the ways that schools, children and parents might use them. Taken together, these strategies shift students' focus towards efficient learning and a deepening awareness of the learning process.

Further reading

To find out more about some of the topics covered in this chapter, here are some suggestions for further reading:

» An excellent web resource for evidence-based learning strategies is the Learning Scientists website, www.learningscientists.org/. It's run by scientists who study learning and memory specifically to help people understand the science and to suggest strategies for how to apply it.

» *The Writing Revolution* by Judith C. Hotchman and Natalie Wexler (2017) is a great book if you are looking for learnable strategies to break down the process of writing essays.

» A really good book for teachers, but which is accessible and readable for parents too, is *The Teaching Rainforest* by Tom Sherrington (2017), an educational consultant and former headteacher. It outlines and explains many of the strategies in this chapter from the perspective of teachers.

Bibliography

Carter, J F and Van Matre, N H (1975) Note Taking versus Note Having. *Journal of Educational Psychology*, 67: 900.

Hochman, J C and Wexler, N (2017) *The Writing Revolution: A Guide to Advancing Thinking Through Writing in All Subjects and Grades*. San Francisco, CA: Jossey-Bass.

Sherrington, T (2017) *The Learning Rainforest: Great Teaching in Real Classrooms*. Melton, Woodbridge: John Catt Educational Ltd.

6. PRIMARY EDUCATION

Key information

- Primary-age children are still developing very quickly, and this introduces more complexity into the learning process. Schools must create curriculums that support personal and academic development in tandem.
- While a wide range of pedagogies and teaching styles are practised in primary education, the most effective for academic instruction involve an element of teacher-led instruction and focus on a systematic curriculum with regular assessment. However, this does not have to be to the exclusion or detriment of collaboration, socialisation and play.
- Teaching literacy requires careful initial instruction in the sound structures of words, but as a child develops as a reader, helping them to read widely and regularly becomes the focus.

You will probably never be more involved with your child's education that when they are in primary school. A local primary school is a local community where parents play an active role, helping on school trips and with fund raising. But what do we know about effective primary education? In this chapter we explore the following questions.

1. What is a curriculum?
2. Do primary school children learn differently from older children?
3. Should primary school children learn through play and discovery?
4. Should students do homework in primary school?
5. Do children do too many tests in primary school?
6. Why is it so important to teach children to read and what are the best ways of doing it?

Question 1: What is a curriculum?

Before looking at some of the distinctive features of how primary-age children learn, it is helpful to acknowledge the importance of the curriculum that they follow. The curriculum is at the heart of any school and, since the advent of Ofsted's new inspection framework in 2019, it has become an increasingly hot topic. The curriculum is *what* is studied, the sequence in which it is studied and how it all fits together. Probably the most useful metaphor to think about the curriculum is as a kind of story.

In films and books, we're used to stories being pieced together carefully to lead us to some point of revelation – an 'Ah ha!' moment when we bring together what previously appeared as only loosely connected facts and plotlines. Without all the build-up of detail and background information, that 'Ah ha!' moment of revelation makes little or no sense. Imagine watching the final hour of *Game of Thrones* without seeing the 62.5 hours that came before it – characters, plots, locations and actions would make no sense, and the enjoyment of the whole narrative working together would be lost.

The idea of a curriculum as a story shows that there is value not just in the main storyline itself, but also in all of the carefully-ordered and well-crafted 'subplots' and background information that help us make sense of the main event. The curriculum that your child encounters in primary school is just one part of the story that they will carry through into secondary school and beyond.

To children, the effects of a well-designed and carefully implemented curriculum can be hugely powerful, as former Cambridge University academic Christine Counsell (2018) points out:

A curriculum exists to change the pupil, to give the pupil new power. One acid test for a curriculum is whether it enables even lower-attaining or disadvantaged pupils to clamber in to the discourse and practices of educated people, so that they gain the powers of the powerful.

Summary

The primary curriculum can usefully be thought of as the important knowledge and skills - brought together as a form of story - that we want our children to learn. The curriculum they experience in primary school should connect to and form the foundation of the secondary school curriculum (which we'll look at in the next chapter).

Question 2: Do primary school children learn differently from older children?

Primary-age children are in an earlier developmental stage than secondary-age children, and this presents a host of challenges for primary school teachers. Primary-age children are:

- **more varied in development and ability than secondary-age children.** This is due to the greater relative variation in their ages and the fact that variances in social background will have more profound impact at that age.
- **lacking the self-sufficiency of older children.** Some children come to primary skill unable to use a toilet or hold their bladders. They will need help tying shoelaces, reading clocks and organising themselves.
- **still learning basic social skills.** Children are still learning how to speak to adults, regulate their own behaviour in public or engage with social conventions like politeness.
- **less able to cope with adult experiences such as pressure and boredom.** Young children are less able to maintain attention for an extended period and are more prone to distraction from boredom.

Primary school teachers must manage not only academic development, but social and emotional development as well (this is, of course, also true to some extent in secondary school, but it is much more acute in primary-age children). Children also develop *across* the school years as well. A five-year-old is very developmentally different from an eight year-old.

The summer birthday effect

The age your child starts school at matters a *lot*. The younger children are within a school year, the lower their subsequent academic achievement is likely to be (Crawford et al, 2007), and this effect is not restricted to their primary education, it can persist all the way to university (Dhuey and Bedard, 2006). It is not hard to understand why this is the case. A child who is four years old for the majority of their first year of school is significantly less cognitively advanced than a child who turns five as they start it. A comparable gap as they leave school would be that of an 18-year-old against a 14-year-old. If they start behind, they can continue to remain behind, with the gap widening over time.

All this can seem very scary to a parent who has a child with a July or August birthday, but it is important to remember that this is *on average*, rather than a specific forecast for individuals. Nevertheless, you may wish to anticipate and even take steps to offset this by looking at the support you can provide at home and asking what policies the school has to support children with late birthdays.

This effect may be particularly acute in the UK due to the relatively early age children start primary school. English children start school in their fifth year while most developed countries wait until they are six or even seven. This summer birthday effect seems to be fairly universal across countries and education systems (Bell et al, 2009).

Summary

Primary school children have greater need for social and emotional development than secondary school children. Effective primary schools carefully plan an integrated sequence of developmental and academic learning that ensures children develop personal and academic skills in tandem - each one supporting the development of the other.

Question 3: Should primary school children learn through play and discovery?

Beliefs about how to teach primary education largely fall into two broad camps – either a child learns through their own experience via play and discovery, or they are guided to learn through a teacher's instruction. The play and discovery approaches have many different names and styles, the most common of which are:

- active learning;
- guided discovery learning;
- enquiry-based learning;
- project-based learning;
- co-operative and collaborative learning;
- experiential learning;
- problem-based learning.

What these approaches have in common is that they all focus on the child learning through personal experience. Advocates for these experiential forms of learning argue that young children are inherently curious – a position formulated by the famous developmental psychologist Jean Piaget (1923) – and therefore they learn better through experience and play than by instruction from a teacher.

While personal experience, play and discovery are naturally a part of most primary school classrooms, the evidence suggests that child shouldn't be given total autonomy over the learning process. Play can have useful effects in social development and engaging young children in learning, but unmediated discovery learning doesn't have much ability to develop skills, and the most effective mechanism for academic learning in primary school is still instruction (Stockard et al, 2018) and feedback (Hattie and Timperley, 2007), sequenced into a meaningful curriculum. An experienced teacher remains far and away the most effective way of delivering that. While primary children do also need careful attention to their emotional and physical development, this is all the more reason to have a teacher there to balance and sequence those elements together.

Summary

Play and discovery are both important elements of the primary school experience, but they should not be used exclusively to deliver academic content. They work most effectively when part of a well-designed curriculum, accompanying a core of teacher-led instruction and feedback.

Question 4: Should students do homework in primary school?

The evidence is very mixed on the effectiveness of homework at primary age (Education Endowment Foundation, 2020) even though the positive impact of homework is clear in secondary school. Leaving aside the moral question of whether children should be given the pressure of homework from so young an age, there are plenty of practical reasons why primary school homework is less effective than it is in secondary school.

- Young learners lack the self-regulation and organisational skills necessary to effectively manage homework.
- They are so varied in their development because of age and background that any positive impact is unevenly distributed between learners.
- Young learners lack the knowledge, motivation and learning skills to study independently.
- Most other things a child will be doing (playing, interacting with parents) are developmentally important as well.

There is some evidence that primary homework can be effective if it is limited, purposeful and relevant. But this is not an argument for universal homework at primary age, and if your child's school does set homework, it is important to be on the lookout for work that seems irrelevant or unnecessarily time-consuming.

Summary

There is mixed evidence that homework is effective at primary school. If employed, it should be purposeful and relevant, and no more time-consuming than it needs to be.

Question 5: Do children do too many tests in primary school?

It is worth remembering here the Bananarama Principle: *it's not what assessment you do, but the way that you do it.* Ultimately, it is not a matter of the amount of assessment, but how it is carried out. Assessment is an essential component of effective primary education, but most of the assessment that takes place in primary school should be continual, for the benefit of the teacher, and in most cases will not be experienced as a test by the children at all. Assessment at primary school can mean activities such as:

- questioning and dialogue;
- looking at students' work;
- tests (usually without drawing any attention to the fact they are tests);

- games;
- songs;
- group activities.

Good primary school teachers will use assessment to assess how children understand and use knowledge, but also use it to shape the learning the child does in future. For example, if you are teaching children to tell the time on the hands of a clock, then you need to know what prior knowledge they have (numbers, awareness of time, etc) in order to be able to teach them effectively.

The debate about formal examinations is more controversial and not easily resolved with research evidence. There remains a healthy debate in the media as to the impact of the formal Key Stage assessments which children sit at the end of Year 2. England is relatively rare in having national assessments at a primary school age, and critics have suggested that these exams encourage schools to put pressure on students to succeed at an age when they are not emotionally capable of dealing with it. Others point to the necessity of having standardised assessments to allow differences in school and student performance to be revealed and changes to be made where necessary to support struggling students. Ultimately, assessments are not inherently harmful, but they can be done in a harmful way.

Summary

Assessment is an essential part of teaching primary-age children, but the best kind of assessment is almost invisible to the students themselves and is woven into their enjoyment of the classroom. Assessment should not be feared by parents, teachers or students, but it must be done properly.

Question 6: Why is it so important to teach children to read and what are the best ways of doing it?

There is a fierce debate about the best way to teach reading that is often referred to in education circles as 'the phonics debate' or, more dramatically, as 'the reading wars'. The question both sides are answering is as follows: *To what extent should teaching focus on the sound structures of English when learning to read?*

One side believes that decoding the symbols into sounds is only part of the puzzle, and that children should be encouraged to adopt other techniques such as recognising the word on sight, guessing it from context and other visual clues – this is often called a **whole-word** approach. The other side argues that a different approach called **systematic synthetic phonics** is the correct method for reading instruction, because it focuses on the skill of decoding the letters into sounds above anything else. It is often referred to simply as 'phonics', which is problematic because many other things are sometimes labelled phonics when they are not the same thing, such as *embedded phonics* and *analytic phonics*, which rely on other strategies besides decoding.

Essentially, synthetic phonics is unique because it is the only approach that uses the sounds of the word, and *only* the sounds of the word, to decode the word. All other approaches encourage kids to guess based upon their wider linguistic knowledge. Guessing the meaning of a new word by using your wider word knowledge can be an effective strategy if you have a lot of prior language knowledge, but it can be completely ineffective if you do not. It will work well if you are a child who has been read to from an early age but can be completely ineffective if you have little or no knowledge of language. The evidence shows that to help *all* children to learn to read, schools must focus on explicitly teaching children how to decode words by using the symbols to work out the sound of the word.

If the evidence in favour of synthetic phonics is strong, why does it remain controversial?

Some critics question whether the evidence is as robust as most believe and you can make the case that systematic phonics has had limited success when implemented as national policy (Bowers, 2020). Others say that whatever the evidence says about its efficacy, the rush to embrace synthetic phonics has had unintended consequences, such as:

- making reading mechanical and less fun, leading to a disengagement with reading for pleasure;

- reducing learning reading to just measuring phonetic ability;

- encouraging teachers to focus exclusively on phonological training and neglect general engagement with literacy;

- it can seem pointless to put literate children through phonics training, although there is no evidence that it is harmful.

This controversy has been stoked further by the introduction of the phonics screening check, a national test in England for all six-year-olds in which their phonological knowledge is assessed. This has proved controversial because some people object to assessing children in national tests at such an early age.

HOW SHOULD WE TEACH CHILDREN TO READ?

While teaching synthetic phonics is an essential strategy for helping children to read, it is not the whole process. In Castles et al's seminal paper 'Ending the Reading Wars' (2018) they argue that different stages of the reading process require a different focus and approach. Early in the process, the focus should be on synthetic phonics and children must be explicitly taught to decode words from the symbols and sounds. However, as children become confident in this skill, the emphasis should focus on the *experience* of reading and the acquisition of supporting knowledge.

Learning to decode

Children first experience books as passengers on a reading journey, dependent on the reading skills of parents and unable to decode words for themselves. This introduction familiarises them with books and the whole idea of writing as a learnable code (Chall, 1983). Children begin the process of learning to read by learning the individual sounds of English (called **phonemes**) and the symbols that are used to represent those phonemes. Initially, this may just be in the form of learning the names of the letters, or by learning their alphabet, but once they know the constituent parts they need to be trained in how to use them to decode full words.

In whole-word reading approaches, children use some phonetic knowledge combined with other cues to guess the most likely word. Cues can include things like the similarity of the word to other words they know, or contextual cues, such the use of pictures. In systematic phonics, however, children are taught that they can derive the sound of a word from the symbols alone. In order to do this they are taught to **segment** words, which means to break them down into their constituent sounds by looking at the symbols. They are then encouraged to **blend** those sounds up into the whole word.

Developing word reading

The obvious criticism of synthetic phonics is that being able to assemble the word from its constituent sounds is not enough for a child to understand that word and use it fluently. What is the point of knowing how to decode the word 'zebra' if you don't know what one is, and you lack the wider knowledge to put it in the context of a sentence? In fact, far from being opposite approaches, decoding sounds and building word comprehension knowledge are two halves of a whole. One requires the other to be useful, and this is an idea often summarised as 'the simple view of reading' (Hoover and Gough, 1990). However, rather than thinking of them as parallel skills, it might be better to think of them as a sequence; as children master decoding, then teachers and parents need to switch the focus from phonics to the experience of reading. As Castles et al explain, '*the single most effective pathway to fluent word reading is print experience: Children need to see as many words as possible, as frequently as possible*' (2018, p 26). This is where advocates of whole-word approaches may have a point when they talk about creating an environment which helps children love reading and which surrounds them with reading experiences. Children who are put into a rich reading environment, and who have the motivation and opportunity to read widely and consume a huge vocabulary of words and their meanings, rapidly develop their reading ability.

The role of the school at this point is to assist the child as they acquire word knowledge. This means strategies such as:

- providing opportunities for both guided and independent reading;
- modelling vocabulary to children;
- explaining new words when they are introduced and used in class;
- teaching vocabulary and assessing children's comprehension of language.

Teachers can also improve students' comprehension skills by:

- explicitly teaching the underlying structures of words such as their history (etymology) and groupings;
- teaching about how the context of different words affects their meanings.

Reading for comprehension

Once children have developed a functionally broad vocabulary and word recognition, they are able to access the wider world of knowledge through reading. They can, to some extent, be 'let loose' on the world of reading. However, there remain some barriers to how well they can read. The most obvious of these is their personal knowledge and understanding of the world. As texts grow more linguistically complex, they tend to demand a greater knowledge of whatever it is the text is about in order for a child to understand them. For example, if a child is given a book about Ancient Rome to read, it may help them to learn about the Romans, but in order to access that knowledge they also need to have some baseline of knowledge to be able to read it in the first place. A child who doesn't know what an *amphitheatre* is, or a *mosaic*, or that the Romans conquered England, may struggle to understand the text, even if they recognise the majority of the words.

Developing this relevant knowledge is a tricky thing given the enormous range and span of texts that children may encounter, but it remains an essential thing for teachers to try to do. Strategies they might employ include:

- planning reading and learning alongside one another in the curriculum, so children may learn about a particular piece of history alongside reading texts about them;
- reading difficult texts together, with the teacher explaining and teaching the supporting information and vocabulary.

WHAT CAN I DO TO HELP AT HOME?

In his excellent book *The Reading Mind*, the psychologist Daniel Willingham (2017) says that parents should avoid using extrinsic rewards like snacks, stickers or cash to incentivise reading. These teach children that reading is without intrinsic value and something that requires compensation, and is thus to be endured, not loved. He also suggests that all strategies should address one of two needs. Either they should maximise the value children gain from reading, or they should make the choice to read easy. Children won't read unless it is an easy and normal choice for them to do so, and they can perceive a personal value from doing it. The following list is a compilation of strategies to help achieve this at home.

Have a culture of reading in the house. Children for whom reading is normalised tend to be much more likely to read for themselves. You could try:

- family reading time;
- curating a family library;
- getting library cards and letting them choose books each week.

Read with children to help them tackle more difficult texts. While reading independently is an important component for building a child's reading skill, there can be a danger that they stick to what they know. One of the most effective ways this can be overcome is to introduce children to more difficult texts and read them together. You could try:

- recommending books for children that are a manageable challenge;
- co-reading a more difficult book, explaining new words and ideas as you go;
- getting library cards and help them explore difficult texts.

Play vocabulary games. Children need to be immersed in the world of words and explore the connections between them. You could try:

- rhyming games to encourage children to understand the phonological relationships between words;
- synonym games that encourage children to think of the relationships between words;
- listening to podcasts and spoken word radio shows together to build up general knowledge.

Encourage reading non-fiction texts. The power of well-chosen non-fiction texts is twofold: first, they often contain certain kinds of challenging vocabulary and world knowledge that novels often lack; second, they expose children to important non-fiction genres (opinion articles, diaries, travel writing, etc) that they cannot gain familiarity with through stories alone. You could try:

- reading the newspaper with children (physical editions can be very useful for this);
- providing non-fiction companion texts for whatever fiction the children are reading. For example, if they are reading *Alice's Adventures in Wonderland*, you could provide them with an encyclopaedia entry on Lewis Carroll.

Engage children in discussions of what they are reading. Helping them to remember the book will help to lock it better in memory, and appropriate questioning can encourage children to reflect on the information in the book and connect it to other things they know or have read. You could try asking:

- What did you like about the book?
- How does the book compare to other books?
- If you met the central character in the book in real life, would you like them?

Summary

Reading skills underpin all other forms of learning and are therefore a major focus for learning in primary school. The best forms of literacy teaching start by using synthetic phonics approaches to build up awareness of the sound/symbol code in English, then progress to broadening word knowledge and encouraging personal reading. Other approaches to decoding words are less effective than synthetic phonics and will widen gaps in achievement.

Ask a teacher

Christopher Such is a teacher and senior leader at Fulbridge Academy in Peterborough. He tweets under the handle @Suchmo83 and his Primary Colours blog can be found at https://primarycolour.home.blog/

In your opinion, what are the biggest challenges of teaching primary-age children?

Many of the most significant challenges of primary teaching correspond to those of secondary teaching: managing difficult behaviour; adapting learning to accommodate the vast range of experiences and capabilities that children bring with them into the classroom; the stress and anxiety of communicating with large groups of unpredictable human beings for long periods. Nevertheless, there are some challenges that are unique to primary schools, or at least that are amplified within them. First, teaching the same group of children for all lessons, as most primary class teachers do, places a particular strain on mutual patience and the relationships that sustain it. This also means that primary teachers tend to work more closely with parents than their secondary counterparts, and the pressures of acting as a surrogate parent are sometimes felt more sharply due to the added vulnerability of young children. Second, as teachers of the entire curriculum, primary educators need to have significant pedagogical knowledge for every subject. A teacher who is tone deaf and has little rhythm will – at some point in their career – still have to find a way to teach music that develops children's abilities and enhances their understanding of the subject. The ideal primary teacher needs to be proficient in mental multiplication, creative writing, singing, drawing, map reading, storytelling and understanding the grand sweep of history and the world's major religions. Such versatility is rare and means that primary teachers have to regularly operate outside of their intellectual comfort zone. Naturally, these challenges are more than offset by the joys of working with young children.

What are the most controversial issues in primary education and to what extent have they been resolved by research evidence?

To my mind, the most controversial issue in education relates to children's first few years in school. Children arrive at vastly different stages of their physical and cognitive development.

The differences can be profound between a child from a supportive, nurturing environment and another child who, for whatever reason, has had a difficult start to life. In many cases these initial disadvantages become entrenched in the first years of primary school through no direct fault of primary school teachers or even school leaders, but through the inevitable pressures of teaching such a broad curriculum ready for assessments at the end of Key Stage 1. For too many children, the foundations of 12 years of formal education are hastily assembled, leaving gaps that impede later learning. The increasing acceptance of the need for systematic phonics instruction – and thorough interventions for those that struggle – has gone some way to ameliorating this issue in early reading, but this is not the case for the rest of the curriculum.

What sorts of things do you think a primary school curriculum should focus on?

The general outline of what is to be taught is outlined by the national curriculum. Nevertheless, this still leaves individual schools a great deal of choice in the range of knowledge and skills to be taught and in the teaching methods employed. Deciding what should go into an effective curriculum depends on the intended aims of that curriculum. Broadly speaking, I believe that the content of a curriculum should align with the aim of supporting children to live fulfilling, successful lives and sharing the accumulated knowledge of humankind that is every child's birth right. This requires the carefully sequenced teaching of foundational knowledge and skills upon which all subsequent learning will be built, not just for its practical employment, but because the knowledge and skills themselves are worth learning for their own sake.

Do you think homework should be set in primary school and if so what should it look like?

There is currently scant evidence that homework at primary level has an impact on learning outcomes. Nevertheless, most schools – due to the expectations of parents, the fear of Ofsted and the inertia of tradition – continue to set homework. My personal view from over a decade in primary teaching is that homework often leads to the fostering of bad habits, particularly in relation to handwriting and spelling. Every minute dedicated to the completion of school tasks at home is a minute that would be better spent playing board games, having conversations and enjoying time together. Of course, there are exceptions to this: children regularly reading to their parents is essential, and the memorisation of useful number facts, such as number bonds and times tables, can be undertaken with immediate feedback that ensures that bad habits are not formed. In short, however, beyond reading and the development of basic maths knowledge, I wouldn't consider myself an advocate of homework for primary-age children.

Has studying research changed how you teach speaking and literacy skills?

Research into reading strongly suggests that speaking skills and literacy are intertwined. Long before the end of primary school, the sentence structures and vocabulary that children encounter in the books they read outstrips that which they will encounter in daily conversation, even with educated adults. This means that the development of independent reading is an essential part of developing children's spoken language and one about which a great deal of research has been undertaken. Beyond the systematic teaching of phonics, reading fluency can be taught in a way that aligns with evidence and allows for comprehension. In particular, fluency practice, where children repeatedly read aloud a given text until they can read it with the accuracy, automaticity and rhythm of a mature reader, has been shown to improve outcomes related to comprehension, the ultimate aim of reading. Equally, research suggests that the development of background knowledge – that which a rich, varied curriculum provides – is an essential component of learning to read and thus also the development of spoken language. When one teaches history, geography, etc, one is also teaching literacy regardless of whether a child is reading or writing in that lesson.

What can parents do at home to help their children succeed at primary school?

The most important support that a parent can offer is the values they promote to their children about the importance of education. Inevitably, much of the learning that children undertake at school will be frustrating, challenging and less innately interesting than whatever hobbies the children enjoy in their free time. Parents who help their child to appreciate this fact – and to take pride in the incremental development of their academic abilities – support them in making the most of the gift of education.

Conclusion

Young children are more varied in their abilities and cognitive development than older children. While teachers need to accommodate the developmental needs of children, and create an enjoyable learning environment, it is a mistake to think that young children can learn from play and discovery alone. Teachers have a critical role in instructing and guiding children and will use the same core teaching mechanisms as you would expect with older children – assessment, feedback and instruction – but they can look different when done with younger learners. In particular, reading is a critical skill, and one that responds best to systematic instruction in phonetics and vocabulary, combined with an environment rich in reading experiences.

❖ What to talk about on parents' evening

- **Curriculum.** The best place to start when investigating a potential primary school or on that first get-to-know-you parents' evening is to ask questions about the school curriculum. How do they teach the core subjects? What do they teach as their foundation subject choices and how do they teach them? How does the learning fit together?

- **Literacy.** Ask about the process of how they teach reading. How do they approach teaching the code of English and the supporting vocabulary? How do they link oral development to written development? How do they refine writing skills and handwriting?

- **Age differences in children.** This will be particularly important if you have a summer-born child, but it is worth asking about regardless as it indicates how much emphasis the school puts on dealing with this difficult issue. Are teachers training to examine and anticipate this phenomenon? Are there additional teaching resources or support available?

further reading

» The synthetic phonics advocate Stephen Parker has written several free ebooks on the subject, including an excellent one for parents. They explore the arguments for synthetic phonics in a simple and accessible way, while also giving loads of great tips for how parents can help this process at home. You can download them at www.parkerphonics.com/.

» *Reading Reconsidered* by Doug Lemov, Colleen Driggs and Erica Woolway (2016) is a superb book about evidence-based approaches to reading. It is aimed at teachers but is very accessible and contains loads of advice and guidance which you can use at home.

Bibliography

Bell, J F, Sykes, E and Vidal, C (2009) Birthdate Effects: A Review of the Literature from 1990-on. [online] Available at: www.cambridgeassessment.org.uk/images/109784-birthdate-effects-a-review-of-the-literature-from-1990-on.pdf (accessed 15 February 2021).

Bowers, J S (2020) Reconsidering the Evidence that Systematic Phonics Is More Effective than Alternative Methods of Reading Instruction. *Educational Psychology Review*, 32: 681-705.

Castles, A, Rastle, K and Nation, K (2018) Ending the Reading Wars: Reading Acquisition from Novice to Expert. *Psychological Science in the Public Interest*, 19: 5-51.

Chall, J S (1983) *Stages of Reading Development*. New York: McGraw-Hill.

Counsell, C (2018) The Dignity of the Thing. [online] Available at: https://thedignityofthethingblog.wordpress.com/author/christinecounsell/ (accessed 15 February 2021).

Crawford, C, Dearden, L and Meghir, C (2007) *When You Are Born Matters: The Impact of Date of Birth on Child Cognitive Outcomes in England*. London: Institute for Fiscal Studies.

Dhuey, E and Bedard, K (2006) The Persistence of Early Childhood Maturity: International Evidence of Long-Run Age Effects. *Quarterly Journal of Economics*, 121: 1437-72.

Education Endowment Foundation (2020) Homework (Primary). [online] Available at: https://educationendowmentfoundation.org.uk/evidence-summaries/teaching-learning-toolkit/homework-primary/ (accessed 15 February 2021).

Hattie, J and Timperley, H (2007) The Power of Feedback. *Review of Educational Research*, 77: 81–112.

Hoover, W A and Gough, P B (1990) The Simple View of Reading. *Reading and Writing*, 2: 127–60.

Lemov, D, Driggs, C and Woolway, E (2016) *Reading Reconsidered: A Practical Guide to Rigorous Literacy Instruction*. San Francisco, CA: Jossey Bass.

Piaget, J (1923) *The Language and Thought of the Child*. London: Psychology Press.

Stockard, J, Wood, T W, Coughlin, C and Rasplica Khoury, C (2018) The Effectiveness of Direct Instruction Curricula: A Meta-Analysis of a Half Century of Research. *Review of Educational Research*, 88: 479–507.

Willingham, D T (2017) *The Reading Mind: A Cognitive Approach to Understanding How the Mind Reads*. New York: John Wiley & Sons.

Young, T and Thomas, M (2014) *What Every Parent Needs to Know: How to Help Your Child Get the Most Out of Primary School*. Harmondsworth: Penguin.

WHAT EVERY PARENT SHOULD KNOW ABOUT EDUCATION

7. SECONDARY SCHOOLS AND COLLEGES

Key information

- Mixed-ability classes in secondary schools offer a small academic advantage to the most able, but this is outweighed by the larger negative effects on others who have not yet achieved as highly.
- Homework can be an effective part of secondary school and college education, but the quality, intensity and focus matter more than the length of time spent on it.
- Between one and two hours of homework per day is optimal for most secondary school children.
- The value of qualifications is highly personal and subjective, although certain A levels are associated with higher earnings in later life.
- Further education offers a range of challenging, meaningful and valuable courses and qualifications.
- A level subjects are equally weighted, but some are more difficult than others.

In England, your child's compulsory full-time education begins in the school term immediately after their fifth birthday, and ends on the last Friday in June of the school year they turn 16 years old (the rules are slightly different in Scotland, Wales and Northern Ireland). Time flies! During this time, some parents choose to educate their child at home, but if you're one of the majority whose child attends a secondary school, what will they study? And what options are open to them after the age of 16?

To help you understand more about your child's education after they leave primary school at age 11, and to support your collaboration with their secondary school, we'll answer the following questions.

1. What is the national curriculum for secondary school children?
2. Do mixed-ability classes affect how children learn?
3. Should students do homework in secondary school and college?
4. Are some qualifications more valuable than others?
5. Are there any differences between colleges and schools when it comes to studying A levels?
6. How do I get my child into a good university?

In doing so, we'll set out some of the key facts about secondary schooling and post-16 education and look at what some of the relevant research evidence tells us.

Question 1: What is the national curriculum for secondary school children?

In secondary schools – as in primary schools – children are expected to experience a 'broad and balanced' curriculum which is ambitious and which prepares them well for the next stage of their life, be that in education or in employment. Of utmost importance is that the teachers in your child's secondary school understand your child as a whole person – their interests, their motivations, the things they struggle with, how they see themselves and others, their ability to stick at things (or not!) when they struggle, the gaps in their knowledge and the skills they have developed. By knowing your child well, and by having a clear and well-developed curriculum, teachers can begin to do what they do best: help your child plug the gaps, light the fires of curiosity, and support them to learn new and more challenging material.

Your child's secondary school curriculum should help them develop independence, resilience and confidence; it should also support them in developing and maintaining good physical and mental health. Such factors are, however, clearly not the sole responsibility of a school; the interplay between what happens at home and what happens at school is crucial, and well-served by strong communications between you, your child, and your child's teachers.

State-funded schools must teach children the knowledge required to achieve the outcomes set out in the national curriculum, or offer something that is of similar or greater ambition and quality. The national curriculum is best seen not as the whole curriculum (the narrative of knowledge that children learn over the course of their education), but as the foundation for what each child should know and be able to do. School leaders and teachers then create sequences of lessons over weeks, terms and years that build on these foundations and address the specific needs of children in the community they serve (for instance, planning opportunities for them to learn about local industrial heritage and its impact on the community's population over time).

In secondary schools, the national curriculum is divided into two sections called Key Stage 3 (Years 7–9) and Key Stage 4 (Years 10 and 11).

KEY STAGE 3 SUBJECTS

The compulsory national curriculum subjects that all secondary schools must teach children between Year 7 and Year 9 (Key Stage 3) are:

- English;
- maths;
- science;
- history;
- geography;
- modern foreign languages;
- design and technology;
- art and design;
- music;
- physical education (PE);
- citizenship;
- computing.

Alongside these subjects, schools must provide both religious education (RE) and relationships and sex education (RSE) (we'll look at these in more detail later) during Key Stage 3.

KEY STAGE 4 SUBJECTS

In Key Stage 4 (Years 10 and 11), there is a noticeable shift in the atmosphere of many secondary schools as teachers and children begin to focus in on the GCSE exams that conclude this phase of education for most children. Children must study the 'core' subjects of English, maths and science, alongside the 'foundation' subjects of computing, PE and citizenship. RE and RSE are also compulsory at Key Stage 4. Your child's school must also offer at least one of the following subjects: art; design and technology; humanities; modern foreign languages.

Children studying science will either take GCSE exams in one or more of biology, chemistry and physics, or they will sit the combined science exams (essentially, one qualification that is the equivalent of two GCSEs). The decision about which qualification exam they will be entered for is one that your school should discuss with your child and you.

THE EBACC

You may also hear about something called the 'EBacc' or English Baccalaureate – this is a collection of GCSEs in English language and literature, maths, the sciences, history or geography, and a language. The government describes the EBacc as '*a way to measure how many pupils in a school choose to take a GCSE*' in this group of subjects; some have criticised it as a means of incentivising certain subjects over others, leading to a decrease in the perceived place and importance of non-EBacc subjects (such as drama).

RELATIONSHIPS AND SEX EDUCATION

As already mentioned, from September 2020 relationships and sex education (RSE) must be on the curriculum in your child's school from the age of 11 onwards. Your child's school must have a written policy made freely available to you (this is most likely to be found on the school's website) and you should familiarise yourself with this, especially if you have concerns about the topics covered or how they are taught, and are considering withdrawing your child from the non-compulsory aspects of RSE.

RELIGIOUS EDUCATION

Similarly to relationships and sex education, schools are required by the government to teach religious education (RE), but you can choose to withdraw your child for all or part of the lessons, also. Your local council is responsible for the content of the RE curriculum; the exception to this is faith schools and academies, which can make their own decisions autonomously.

If you do have concerns about either RSE or RE, make a point of arranging a conversation with the relevant teacher or leader in your child's school. Keeping the dialogue open will allow you, your child and their teachers to make the best decision, and will ensure that the school is able to make appropriate plans, should your child not attend certain lessons.

CULTURAL CAPITAL

The concept of 'cultural capital' is not a new one (the French sociologist Pierre Bourdieu wrote extensively on the topic in the 1960s and 1970s), but it has recently taken on a new prominence in English schools as a result of the revised national curriculum and Ofsted's rewriting of their inspection handbook.

Going to school should – under the most recent changes to the national curriculum and Ofsted's regulatory framework (Ofsted, 2019a) – help all children to develop cultural capital. This is described by Ofsted as the '*essential knowledge that pupils need to be educated citizens, introducing them to the best that has been thought and said, and helping to engender an appreciation of human creativity and achievement*' (Ofsted, 2019b).

Saying that inspectors will consider as part of their judgements the extent to which a school equips its students with both essential knowledge and cultural capital is a feature of the regulator's work which has come in for criticism from some quarters as a way of advancing '*the idea that some versions of culture are more valuable than others*' (Olah, 2019). Whatever your views on the role of schools in developing cultural capital, however, the ambition to open up as much of the world's cultural life as possible to each and every child is, surely, a laudable one; regardless of a family's resources and background, the place a child lives or the schooling experiences that they have had to date, a considered, wide and varied education should be available to all children so that they are as well-equipped as possible to enter adult life, and to enjoy the rich cultural diversity that surrounds them, and of which they are an integral part.

INCREASING CHALLENGE AND QUALIFICATION REFORM

The early 2010s brought with them a raft of changes in education that saw qualifications like GCSEs increase in difficulty as the government sought to improve the confidence that students, parents, schools and employers had in the qualifications awarded to children at age 16. Increasingly, schools felt pressured to 'teach to the test', and there was a narrowing of the curriculum – in some instances, the curriculum that children were entitled to was gripped so tightly and stripped so far back to its bare bones that it focused only on the topics most likely to appear on a GCSE exam paper (lots of teachers became pretty adept at predicting the types of questions that would appear). Much of the interesting, valuable richness of the curriculum was lost. This sharp focus on achieving the highest grades possible in national exams meant that some of the richness found in a broad and balanced curriculum – richness that develops both deep knowledge and strong cultural capital – was side-lined.

Over a decade on, and GCSEs in England are now based on new and more demanding content: your child is expected to learn more material than many parents experienced during their own secondary school education, and that material is more sophisticated than was tested in many of the GCSEs of old. In response to this, the curricula that schools must design and deliver are themselves more challenging: the expectations placed on both teachers and students have changed significantly.

Alongside changes to the degree of challenge and sophistication of the knowledge and skills that schools are expected to teach your child, GCSE qualifications now have a grading scale that is unfamiliar to some parents: instead of the old letter grades of A*–U, GCSEs are now awarded with a numerical grade between 9 and 1 (9 being the highest). For the sake of comparison, an old 'A' grade is similar to a low grade 7 under the new system; the 'C' grade that was the benchmark for many employers is equivalent to a new grade 4.

Summary

The curriculum has changed significantly in recent years and will likely continue to do so over time; similarly, qualifications such as GCSEs have increased in scope and difficulty. Schools are entrusted to help your child build both their subject knowledge and cultural capital, so that they are equipped for life after school.

Question 2: Do mixed-ability classes affect how children learn?

Policy-makers have long been keen on the idea that grouping children by ability or attainment in classrooms is a way to raise educational standards. Intuitively, many parents also feel that their child should be taught in classes with children of similar levels of ability or attainment. So-called 'setting' and 'streaming' practices have been common in some of England's schools for many decades, but do they offer the best for your child's education? Would a classroom with a mix of children with *different* abilities and attainment levels be better?

According to research published by the Education Endowment Foundation (drawn from studies undertaken over more than 50 years), '*On average, pupils experiencing setting or streaming make slightly less progress than pupils taught in mixed attainment classes*' (EEF, 2018). Averages can be misleading, so what's underneath this 'average finding'?

Digging deeper into the evidence, you find that setting and streaming practices tend to have slight negative effects on lower-attaining learners and on those in the middle of the attainment range, while there is a small positive impact for higher-attaining children: on balance, the research evidence suggests that setting and streaming are not effective ways for schools to help *all* children improve their attainment. The small benefits for those at the upper end of the attainment range are outweighed by the negative effects on other children who have not yet achieved as highly. But there's more to the discussion about setting and streaming than just attainment.

CONFIDENCE

Going to secondary school isn't all about getting grades (although they're clearly of significant importance and, ultimately, form a big part of the 'currency' that will help your child into a course of study or a job that they want to get), so it's interesting to note that setting and streaming may also negatively impact on the confidence, attitudes and engagement of some children, by creating an environment in which they believe that their attainment cannot be improved through effort.

Researchers such as Professor Becky Francis have suggested that '*practices of "ability grouping" reflect cultural investments in discourses of "natural order" and hierarchy*' (Francis et al, 2017) and question why – despite the facts that research has a) failed to find evidence of the benefits of grouping children by ability and b) found disadvantageous effects for some lower-attaining children – ability grouping remains a common practice in some schools today.

It's hard to be swayed by research evidence when gut instinct kicks in: for many parents, setting or streaming feels intuitively right for their child. If, however, you think of education as a community activity in which children participate collectively in ways that benefit both themselves *and* each other, the practices of setting and streaming – which often imply competition and hierarchy, and for which there is very little robust supporting evidence – become highly problematic.

Summary

The topic of mixed ability versus ability grouping can be a heated one in some schools and communities. There is, however, very little evidence that setting and streaming by attainment or ability are likely to improve your child's academic outcomes and confidence, and there is evidence they may even harm them.

Question 3: Should students do homework in secondary school and college?

'Homework' is the word used to describe the tasks that children are expected to complete outside of normal lesson time. Your child might be asked to prepare something for the next lesson, to study for a test, or to consolidate what they have learned by completing a task. Some schools have homework clubs where children can do the work assigned for completion outside of lesson hours.

Like school assemblies and exercise books, homework seems like it has always just 'been there', a non-negotiable, part-of-the-furniture piece of school life. But if we were to think hard and choose what to keep in our child's schooling and what to discard, would homework make the cut, or would it be consigned to history?

In secondary schools, the answer would likely be 'yes' it would make the cut, although it's a 'yes' that comes with strings attached (as you'll have worked out by now, there are rarely any clear-cut answers in education). The research evidence on homework in secondary schools seems to suggest it's most effective when used as an integral, targeted tool for enhancing a child's learning in a particular area.

In 2009, the Canadian Council on Learning published a summary of work they had done to systematically review 18 studies about homework that had been published between 2003 and 2007. Their findings indicated clear trends from the research evidence on homework that they reviewed.

- *Homework that demands active student engagement is likely to be effective.*
- *There is probably an academic benefit to the judicious assignment of homework.*
- *Homework will impact different students differently (older students seem most likely to benefit).*
- *Effort is more important than time.*

Echoing what we found in Chapter 3, homework that actually makes students think hard about something is likely to have an impact, and the volume of it and time spent on it should be considered carefully (more does not always mean better). Yet again, the Bananarama Principle can be helpful here – it's not the volume of homework you do, but the quality, intensity and focus of the task that make the difference.

Homework tasks that are specific and manageable can be really useful: if they offer a level of challenge that your child can cope with (meaning that they have the prior knowledge and the ability to self-regulate as they undertake the tasks), they can add value. Part of the difficulty for teachers in setting really great homework, however, is pitching it at a 'challenge point' where it is manageable, motivating, and challenging (and this, again, is where the power of really great assessment and testing comes to the fore).

HOW LONG SHOULD YOUR CHILD SPEND ON HOMEWORK?

Getting this desirably difficult level of challenge right is one part of good homework, but another key consideration is how long should be spent doing it – as we've seen already, effort is more important than time. The time you have with your child each day is incredibly valuable, so time spent on homework should add value. Real value. When you dig into the research evidence, there isn't a consensus on exactly how long a child in secondary school should spend on homework each day, but some studies indicate that somewhere between one and two hours is optimal for most secondary school-age children (although this is only the case if what is actually being done for homework is an integral part of learning).

Being really clear on the school's homework policy and expectations – and then reinforcing these at home – is an excellent way to support your child's learning. Also, help your child find a quiet, calm place to concentrate on doing their homework, one where distractions (such as mobile phones and TV) are kept to a minimum. And finally, support your child to do their homework (as we mentioned in Chapter 5) but don't do it for them.

Summary

Homework in secondary school can add value to your child's education, but only if it is aligned with the curriculum, and is manageable, motivating and desirably difficult so that hard thinking ensues. For most children and for most of the time, spending between one and two hours each day on their homework is sufficient, although the active effort they put in is more important than the duration. The amount of time that children spend on their homework may well vary during the school year, increasing in the run-up to exams.

Question 4: Are some qualifications more valuable than others?

If we think about nationally recognised qualifications such as GCSEs or A levels as a form of currency, then clearly there is significant value in them; they are used by students, employers, colleges and universities as a means of representing the achievement of a standard (as indicated by the grade or mark awarded), and as a tool for sorting (for instance, when it comes to selecting candidates for a job interview or for places at a university). Qualifications are like a passport; they're not the destination itself, rather they allow the bearer to pass through to begin the next part of their journey.

The value of a qualification, therefore, differs depending on its purpose, or the desired 'destination'. If your child wants to become a medical doctor, qualifications in certain subjects (such as the sciences) will likely be of greater value than those in areas such as drama and history, a fact that does not diminish the value of arts and humanities subjects per se. If your child has little idea about their next steps in life, a broad set of qualifications that keep options open (in terms of future study and employment) is valuable.

Value is a very personal concept. Certain qualifications in certain subjects (take a GCSE in maths, for example) are valuable because of their 'facilitating' role – they allow the bearer of the qualification to move on to do something else. Ultimately, the argument is a highly subjective one, except for when we look at the relationship between certain qualifications (and indeed, institutions) and earnings later in life.

Research evidence indicates that studying for a degree in medicine or dentistry tends to be associated with higher earnings than, for instance, a degree in engineering. People who complete nursing degrees tend to earn more than those who have a creative arts and design degree. That is not to say that dentistry is of greater *value* than pottery; rather, the average income associated with each is different.

For those who do go on to university, it is not just the subject they study that is likely to affect their earnings, but also *where* they study. According to analysis in 2017 from the Institute for Fiscal Studies and reported by the BBC (Britton, 2017), the average yearly earnings for someone who attended the London School of Economics or the University of Oxford are greater than £40,000 five years after graduation; for graduates of the universities in the Russell Group (a self-selected group of 24 research-focused universities perceived by some to represent the best in the UK), the average was £33,500.

Defining the value of any qualification is, ultimately, a personal thing and not one that can – or should – be done in the pages of this book. What we can say with confidence, however, is that research evidence indicates that the more years someone spends in education in any form, the better their health (Feinstein et al, 2006), the more they're likely to earn (Britton et al, 2020) and the less they're likely to commit crime (Groot and van den Brink, 2010). Staying in education is a good thing not just for your child, but for the society in which they live.

Summary

Attaining certain qualifications in secondary school and in post-16 education will make it more likely that a child is able to go on and study a course that leads to higher earnings than otherwise they would have, although this is only one (narrow) way of interpreting the word 'value'. Aside from the utility value associated with qualifications, there are other less tangible but perhaps equally valuable effects of attaining qualifications in a range of areas.

Question 5: Are there any differences between colleges and schools when it comes to studying A levels?

As children approach the conclusion of full-time compulsory education at age 16, they face a set of options for the following two years: some choose to leave school and work or volunteer while in part-time education; some look forward to continuing their studies full-time; and some take on an apprenticeship or traineeship.

For those looking to study A level courses, further education (FE) college presents an alternative to a secondary school's sixth form. And, while students in schools and colleges may have similar experiences of the expectations placed on them around responsible behaviour, attendance and meeting deadlines, there are important differences that are worth considering at this point in a child's education

FURTHER EDUCATION

Further education (FE) colleges receive government funding to provide education and training to people over the age of 16 (some also offer courses for 14 and 15 year-olds), so they are separate from schools and universities. There are five different types of FE provider: colleges, independent training providers (ITPs), local authority (LA) providers, employer providers and third-sector providers.

TYPES OF COLLEGE

General further education (GFE) colleges provide the majority of further education in England and offer a wide range of programmes (from accounting to beauty therapy, health and social care to maths) which often focus on supporting your child to develop workplace skills through technical and professional education and training.

In addition to GFE colleges, **sixth form colleges** focus primarily on education for people aged 16–19. Sixth form colleges are not attached to secondary schools, and the majority of people study full-time academic courses (around two-thirds of sixth form college students go on to study in higher education).

Students attending **land-based colleges** study in areas relating to animals, plants, farming, and the environment (such as agriculture, horticulture, tree surgery and veterinary science) with a combination of hands-on and classroom teaching.

Art, design and performing arts colleges focus on education for those interested in careers in creative industries. These colleges offer entry-level courses, higher education courses and short courses for students of all ages.

National specialist colleges provide specialist support to young people with learning difficulties, disabilities and/or mental health problems, with many offering sensory and therapeutic facilities, and supported work environments.

Secondary schools with sixth forms – by virtue of teaching children under the age of 16 as well as those older students – tend to have a more prescriptive atmosphere than FE colleges (students might be required to wear a uniform, for instance, or may not be allowed to leave the school site during the course of the day). You may find a more relaxed atmosphere in an FE college, with students expected to be on site only during teaching time.

Summary

The atmosphere and environment of a college is likely to be one of the most significant differences for a child coming out of secondary school. Knowing more about the different types of post-16 education available in your area is one way of helping your child find a path that enables them to develop their talents and interests, and to acquire the skills needed for their next steps (to university or work).

Question 6: How do I get my child into a good university?

Many parents want to get their children into a 'good' university, although it can be extremely hard to pin down exactly what that means. British universities are very competitively ranked against each other, in terms of both public reputation and the university ratings systems that are used to help students choose between institutions and courses (THE, 2020). Most parents are aware of the reputations of the most selective institutions, Oxford and Cambridge (collectively known as Oxbridge) and the so-called 'red-brick' traditional universities, some of which are branded together as the Russell Group. There are many different university ratings systems, and they should probably not be used as the single point of data by which your university decision is made. University rankings vary from year to year, and there can often be large discrepancies between the ranking of a department and the ranking of an institution – there are highly ranked departments in lower-ranked universities and vice versa.

While there is plenty of evidence available that attending more selective universities is associated with greater earning potential and career success, it is unclear how much this is a causal relationship. Oxford and Cambridge are free to hoover up the very best and brightest students. Do their graduates go on to successful careers afterwards because of their Oxbridge experience, or were they destined for success anyway?

SUBJECTS DO HAVE DIFFERENT WEIGHTINGS, BUT GRADES ARE VERY IMPORTANT AS WELL

A levels are supposed to be equivalent to each other; an A level in maths should be as challenging as an A level in sociology. The UCAS application process for university treats them as equivalent, giving the same grade in any two subjects an identical amount of points.

However, the education sector has a dirty little secret: some subjects are harder than others. Coe et al (2008) showed that certain subjects, particularly maths and sciences, are much harder to achieve equivalent outcomes in than other subjects. Differences in difficulty lead to differences in perceptions of value, and the most selective universities do tend to give more weight to certain A levels than others. The Russell Group attempted to codify these biases by releasing a list of 'facilitating subjects'. This is a list of those subjects the universities held in highest esteem and were therefore more likely to facilitate access to the most selective universities. While the controversial list has subsequently been withdrawn, it remains a useful guide to the biases of university admissions. The facilitating subjects are:

- English literature;
- history;
- modern and classical languages;
- maths and further maths;

- physics;
- biology;
- chemistry;
- geography.

However, the existence of the different values of individual A levels is not an argument that all students should be taking facilitating subjects. First, difficulty can be subjective; a brilliant mathematician might struggle if they took a textiles A level. Second, the vast majority of degrees and universities are accessible without facilitating subjects and because every A level is worth the same amount of points under the UCAS system, it actually creates an incentive for students to pick subjects not on their value, but on their ability to get high grades in them. This means that, for many students, taking a heavy academic programme may be the wrong decision because it may ultimately result in a student achieving a lower set of results and limiting their university options. The student who achieves three A grades has much better options than one who takes on traditional high-value subjects and ends up only able to achieve two Bs and a C.

HOW DO I HELP MY CHILD CHOOSE THE RIGHT COURSES?

- Start with the end in mind. What do they want to do after university? What sort of level of university is it likely that they will be able to attend? A great place to start is the Informed Choices website (www.informedchoices.ac.uk/) which is run by the Russell Group. Another good thing to do is to check the websites of universities and courses they are interested in. How specific are their subject requirements? What grades do they need?

- If your child is aiming for a very selective university, but doesn't know what they want to study, they should consider taking at least one traditional academic A level that they enjoy and are good at. If your child is not aiming for a highly selective university, then they don't necessarily need to focus on academic A levels, and might consider focusing on picking a combination of subjects that they enjoy and which access university courses they are interested in.
- Not all your child's subjects have to link to their likely degree subjects. Someone who wants to study law at university doesn't have to have studied law at A level. Universities care far less about exact subject combinations than most people think. If your child is heading towards STEM degrees (science, technology, engineering and maths) then, yes, a couple of subjects should be in that area, but otherwise the relative difficulty of the A levels they choose and the grades they can achieve will be more important for securing the right university place for them.

Summary

As with school choice, university choice is often about the 'fit and feel' of a particular course and location, so spending time ascertaining which institutions are available to your child (based on location, the grades required and the funding needed) is important. While some universities and courses are more likely to lead to greater earning potential in the future, success in higher education demands the kind of commitment to learning that is best served by deep interest and passion for a subject area.

❖ What to talk about on parents' evening

- **Know the curriculum.** Talk to your child's teachers to get as clear an idea of the curriculum content in the subject area they teach. Ask them to explain how what they're teaching right now links to what is coming up, and how you can support your child best (perhaps through reading about topics with them, visiting a local landmark or looking at a specific website).

- Ask your child's teachers what approaches and strategies they use to help develop **independence, resilience and confidence.** Some of these will be easy to transfer and use at home, and trying them will help you to work in collaboration with school on some important aspects of development.

- **Think about religious education, and relationships and sex education.** Because you can choose for your child to opt out of some lessons in these areas, you should make sure that you are clear on what is taught in them if you're thinking about making this decision, and on what your child would miss out on if they were not to attend.

- **Talk about your child's interests.** Not every teacher will know your child's interests and passions, so talking about them to their teachers will help them get to know them better. As your child moves through school, this will also help them advise you and your child better on good options after the age of 16. For some, this will be a vocational course in a further education college, for others it will be studying A levels.

further reading

» The Education and Training Foundation has produced a thorough and informative guide to the further education system in England (called *So What is the FE Sector?*), and it's freely available to download at their website (www.et-foundation.co.uk).

Bibliography

Britton, J (2017) The Degrees that Make You Rich... and the Ones that Don't. [online] Available at: www.bbc.co.uk/news/education-41693230 (accessed 15 February 2021).

Britton, J, Dearden, L, van der Erve, L and Waltmann, B (2020) The Impact of Undergraduate Degrees on Lifetime Earnings: Research Report. [online] Available at: https://assets.publishing.service.gov.uk/government/uploads/system/uploads/attachment_data/file/869263/The_impact_of_undergraduate_degrees_on_lifetime_earnings_research_report_ifs_dfe.pdf (accessed 15 February 2021).

Canadian Council on Learning (2009) A Systematic Review of Literature Examining the Impact of Homework on Academic Achievement. [online] Available at: http://en.copian.ca/library/research/ccl/lessons_learning/homework_helps/homework_helps.pdf (accessed 15 February 2021).

Coe, R, Searle, J, Barmby, P, Jones, K and Higgins, S (2008) *Relative Difficulty of Examinations in Different Subjects*. Durham: CEM Centre, Durham University.

Department for Education (2017) Employment and Earnings Outcomes of Higher Education Graduates: Experimental Statistics Using the Longitudinal Education Outcomes (LEO) Data: Further Breakdowns. [online] Available at: www.gov.uk/government/statistics/graduate-outcomes-for-all-subjects-by-university (accessed 15 February 2021).

Dilnot, C (2018) The Relationship Between A Level Subject Choice and League Table Score of University Attended: The 'Facilitating', the 'Less Suitable', and the Counter-Intuitive. *Oxford Review of Education*, 44(1): 118–37.

WHAT EVERY PARENT SHOULD KNOW ABOUT EDUCATION

EEF (2018) Setting and Streaming. [online] Available at: https://educationendowmentfoundation.
org.uk/evidence-summaries/teaching-learning-toolkit/setting-or-streaming/ (accessed 15
February 2021).

Feinstein, L, Sabates, R, Anderson, T M, Sorhaindo, A and Hammond, C (2006) What are the
Effects of Education on Health? In *Measuring the Effects of Education on Health and Civic
Engagement: Proceedings of the Copenhagen Symposium* (pp 171–354). Paris: Organisation for
Economic Co-operation and Development.

Francis, B, Archer, L, Hodgen, J, Pepper, D, Taylor, B and Travers, M C (2017) Exploring the Relative
Lack of Impact of Research on 'Ability Grouping' in England: A Discourse Analytic Account.
Cambridge Journal of Education, 47(1): 1–17.

Groot, W and van den Brink, H M (2010) The Effects of Education on Crime. *Applied
Economics*, 42(3), 279–89.

Ofsted (2019a) Education Inspection Framework. [online] Available at: www.gov.uk/
government/publications/education-inspection-framework/education-inspection-framework
(accessed 15 February 2021).

Ofsted (2019b) School Inspection Update. [online] Available at: https://assets.publishing.
service.gov.uk/government/uploads/system/uploads/attachment_data/file/772056/School_
inspection_update_-_January_2019_Special_Edition_180119.pdf (accessed 15 February 2021).

Olah, N (2019, October 21). Teaching 'Cultural Capital' in Schools is Not the Path to a More
Equal Society. The New Statesman. [online] Available at: www.newstatesman.com/politics/
education/2019/10/teaching-cultural-capital-schools-not-path-more-equal-society (accessed
15 February 2021).

THE (2020) World University Rankings. [online] Available at: www.timeshighereducation.com/
world-university-rankings (accessed 15 February 2021).

8. BEHAVIOUR, STRESS AND MENTAL HEALTH

Key information

- Schools manage behaviour as a way of creating the best possible environment for learning.
- Behaviour and academic outcomes are linked.
- More than 30 per cent of school exclusions are caused by persistent disruptive behaviour.
- The number of fixed-term (non-permanent) exclusions has risen in recent years.
- Stress is a normal human feeling, but frequent or prolonged exposure to it can be very damaging.
- Mental health problems affect a large proportion of children and young people, and timely intervention is key to reducing the risk of long-term effects.

It's normal to feel worried, confused, even helpless when your child is unhappy, has a low mood or feels stressed. You might be concerned about aspects of your child's behaviour or mental health that seem new and out of character and, despite your best efforts, things do not seem to be improving. At this point, platitudes from other people like '*Don't worry, it's just a phase*', or '*There's nothing you can do other be there for them*' can sound hollow; hearing these well-intentioned words can serve only to maintain or even increase the worry and frustration.

In this chapter, we're going to focus on behaviour, stress and mental health, and consider what you can do if you're worried about your child. Alongside the relevant research evidence, we interviewed Rochdale headteacher Janice Allen, and independent education adviser (and Department for Education 'Behaviour Czar') Tom Bennett, and asked them to highlight some of the practical ways teachers and school leaders actively manage behaviour, and promote good mental health in schools.

Here are the questions we answer in this chapter.

1. Why do schools manage behaviour and how do they do it?
2. What happens when a child's behaviour is too challenging for a school's normal behaviour policy and more support is needed?
3. What are the signs of stress?
4. What is good mental health?
5. What can you do to help your child develop good mental health?

Question 1: Why do schools manage behaviour and how do they do it?

Schools manage behaviour because they are communities in and of themselves, and they work well when shared values and guiding principles are respected and adhered to consistently by every member of the community (children, parents, teachers and leaders). As we've already seen, well-managed classrooms and school environments are integral to effective learning, something that government adviser Tom Bennett wrote about in his 2017 *Creating a Culture* report:

Behaviour in school is inseparable from academic achievement, safety, welfare and wellbeing, and all other aspects of learning. It is the key to all other aims, and therefore crucial. Its correct direction is equally crucial, and should be viewed as an issue of the highest strategic importance. Behaviour does not manage itself, except haphazardly.

(Bennett, 2017, p 12)

In managing behaviour, teachers are not trying to repress students or create compliant robots; rather the focus is on building and sustaining a community of learners in a safe and supportive environment, one that helps both individuals and the whole community to flourish. As headteacher Janice Allen puts it *'you've got to get the behaviour right within an environment to enable good teaching and learning to take place'.* And 'getting the behaviour right' is one of the most significant ways in which schools help children and young people develop responsibility for themselves, and for the others around them.

THE EVIDENCE ON BEHAVIOUR AND ACHIEVEMENT

There is a strong relationship between children's behaviour in school and their outcomes both academically and socially: children who are *'not engaged in troublesome behaviours at ages 10 and 13 make more progress in secondary school (i.e. Key Stage 2 to Key Stage 3; Key Stage 3 to Key Stage 4)'* (Morrison Gutman and Vorhaus, 2012). In classrooms where behaviour is generally good, more time is spent learning, teachers' working environment is better, and recruiting new teaching staff to a school is less challenging. Moreover, children with better well-being (those with fewer fears and anxieties, strong friendships and a sense of engagement with school, for instance) tend to make more progress than others (Morrison Gutman and Vorhaus, 2012).

Research commissioned by the Department for Education and conducted by ASK Research found in 2017 that one common theme in schools rated as Outstanding by Ofsted was *'the overarching approach to behaviour management: balancing positive reinforcement and modelling of good behaviours for learning with clearly communicated approaches for dealing with poorer behaviour'* (Skipp and Hopwood, 2017, p 3). Such 'good behaviours' in school are fostered more effectively when the classroom environment is one in which children *want* to behave appropriately, rather than one in which good behaviour has to be enforced. When you visit school and see a classroom in which good behaviour seems to be the norm for children, underpinning that environment will likely be a strong relationship between the teacher and their students, but you'll also find something more concrete and visible: routines and consequences.

ROUTINES AND CONSEQUENCES

It may sound dull and archaic, but school and classroom routines are designed to help both your child and their peers develop habits that help them learn; their importance is such that many schools don't simply make passing reference to them, they actively teach and reinforce them.

In the *Creating a Culture* report for the Department for Education, Tom Bennett (2017, p 31) stated:

Creating school culture is about designing social norms that one would want to see reproduced throughout the school community. Leaders must ask, 'What would I like all students to do, routinely?' 'What do I want them to believe about themselves, their achievements, each other, the school?' Once these questions have been answered, the leader can then translate these aspirations into expectations. Social norms are found most clearly in the routines of the school. Any aspect of school behaviour that can be standardised because it is expected from all students at all times should be, for example walking on the left or right of the corridor, entering the class, entering assembly, clearing tables at lunch. These routines should be communicated to, and practiced by, staff and students until they become automatic. This then frees up time, mental effort and energy towards more useful areas, such as study.

No matter how robust and effective the routine, nor how strong the relationship between teachers and the children in their classroom, things go awry from time to time, and children behave inappropriately. According to Bennett, in these instances, the most useful response by a teacher is to implement an appropriate consequence that has been defined and described to the children in advance, and is understood by them.

To help your child's teachers support your child, ask them what routine behaviours (such as wearing of uniform, listening respectfully when someone else is speaking, or putting away resources and materials once they are finished with) are expected of children. Also, talk to your child about why these routines are helpful for their learning and their peers' learning, ensure that they understand them clearly, and that behaviour below expectation has consequences for them.

SAFE AND SUPPORTED CHILDREN

Behaviour in schools has been a hot topic in English schools for some time. In 2014, Ofsted wrote in their report *Below the Radar* (pp 4–5) that:

The YouGov surveys show that pupils are potentially losing up to an hour of learning each day in English schools because of this kind of disruption in classrooms. This is equivalent to 38 days of teaching lost per year. A large number of pupils, therefore, are being denied a significant amount of valuable learning time. Many teachers have come to accept some low-level disruption as a part of everyday life in the classroom. One fifth of the teachers surveyed indicated that they ignored low-level disruption and just 'tried to carry on.' However, this behaviour disturbs the learning of the perpetrators as well as that of others.

WHAT EVERY PARENT SHOULD KNOW ABOUT EDUCATION

With the potential for children to lose out on valuable teaching time, schools put huge effort into ensuring that children are safe and supported, and that disruptions to learning are minimised. In 2019, Her Majesty's Chief Inspector of schools, Amanda Spielman, wrote that:

Everyone stands to benefit from good behaviour in schools. Effective behaviour management means that low-level disruption is not tolerated and pupils' behaviour does not disrupt lessons or the day-to-day life of the school. Pupils can learn; teachers can teach; staff can do their job; and parents have confidence that their child is safe and supported to do the best that they can.

Many schools actively promote good behaviour through rewards (such as house points or similar) and through open conversations with students about respect for themselves and for others. But what happens when behaviour is deemed inappropriate?

Most 'low-level disruptions' are dealt with in the classroom, with a conversation (to ascertain what happened and how the child is feeling), a recording of the type of unacceptable behaviour incident, and perhaps a sanction; the intention is always to manage a child's behaviour so that they and their peers can learn. To help a child see the connection between an expectation (such as waiting patiently to speak in class) and their action (talking over other children, for example), there has to be a consequence (such as a sanction).

If these initial responses to inappropriate behaviour are unsuccessful, the next step (ideally, already communicated to and understood by the child) will be taken. Every school and college has its own series of steps, but below are a few examples.

- The child leaves the classroom for a period of time to reflect on their behaviour and the consequences of it for them and their peers.
- The child may be sent to see a member of the school's leadership team to discuss their behaviour.
- A learning mentor may work with the child for a specified period of time to help them understand and improve their behaviour.
- In some schools, the child may continue their education for a period of time in a 'school within a school' – a place designed to provide additional support.

This final step – the 'school within a school' – is one way that some schools work intensively with a child to help them address and improve their behaviour. Headteacher Janice Allen is firm in her belief that '*there is a fresh start for everyone*' each day and that '*even if they [the child] have done the most awful thing the day before, you have to look for ways in*' to support their development and growth.

Managing and developing appropriate learner behaviour that actively helps your child is a partnership between you and the school. By keeping good lines of communication between school and home, your child's teachers will be keen to help you know the full picture – the good and the not-so-good – of how things are going, and it's helpful for you to keep them updated in a similar way. Such communication is at the heart of a collaborative approach to helping children learn and grow.

For some children, education in mainstream school proves too great a challenge, and this is the point at which exclusion from school and a different, alternative provision – our next topic – may be considered.

Summary

The school and classroom rules your child's school has are there to help your child learn. Setting out clear routines and consequences for your child is a mainstay of good classroom management, and good classroom management is a foundation for learning. Simply knowing what the routines and consequences are (and reinforcing the school's use of them) is a useful way to understand more and collaborate in your child's education.

Question 2: What happens when a child's behaviour is too challenging for a school's normal behaviour policy and more support is needed?

EXCLUSION FROM MAINSTREAM SCHOOL

Excluding a child from mainstream school is a decision that is never taken lightly. In cases where there are sufficient disciplinary grounds to do so, a headteacher (and only the headteacher) may exclude a child from school for one or more fixed-term periods for up to a maximum of 45 days in a single school year (the average duration is two days); in more serious situations, exclusion may be on a permanent basis. Such permanent exclusion from school is only ever a last resort, and comes from serious breaches of the school's behaviour policy, and in circumstances where the continued presence of the child in school would lead to other children's education being seriously damaged.

According to statistics published by the Department for Education, over 30 per cent of all exclusions from school are for persistent disruptive behaviour; physical assaults to other pupils and to adults account for around 15 per cent of exclusions, with verbal abuse/threatening behaviour against an adult making up a similar proportion.

ALTERNATIVE PROVISION

When Tom Bennett was writing the *Creating a Culture* report on behalf of the UK government in 2017, he found that the most effective schools he saw had places where children could go to receive extra support when they experienced challenging behavioural circumstances – a 'school within a school'. Children struggling to manage their own behaviour can leave the classroom, for the well-being and continuing education of the other children in their class, as well as to receive more nurture, mentoring or counselling as needed. Many schools have some form of this 'halfway house' where they can provide more appropriate levels of support to children who need it, but when this is not sufficient, local authorities and schools can arrange an 'alternative provision' for a child. Alternative provision is education that is delivered outside of the mainstream school setting because of exclusion, illness or other reasons that make mainstream schooling unsuitable.

For those children who have the most severe difficulties in managing their emotions and behaviour, for instance, a Social, Emotional and Mental Health (SEMH) school might be the most appropriate place for them. In other instances, children might attend a Pupil Referral Unit (PRU); in the best of these, Tom Bennett says, you tend to see a lot of tailored, bespoke attention given to therapeutic approaches that simply cannot be provided in a mainstream school setting. He is at pains to point out, however, that such '*boutique education*' should not be equated with a lack of structure and rigour; indeed, teachers and leaders in PRUs work hard to help children address the specific needs they have, and to develop the skills and habits needed to succeed both in and away from the PRU.

Good alternative provision is highly focused on teaching and developing appropriate habits, attitudes, beliefs and values about how to interact with others, and has highly consistent levels of what Bennett calls '*consequential systems*'. While they are not overly punitive, there is a strong 'culture of consequence' in good alternative provision settings, reinforcing the principle that actions matter and have consequences.

IS THE NUMBER OF EXCLUSIONS INCREASING?

Contrary to popular belief, the percentage of children *permanently* excluded across all school types remained fairly stable in the period between 2006 and 2018 (at around 0.1 per cent). Since the 2013/2014 school year, there has been a slight increase in the rate of secondary school exclusions, although the most recently reported figures are still lower than in 2006.

Fixed-period exclusions have, on the other hand, been increasing in recent years (but have fallen in special schools); a rise that is chiefly accounted for by more pupils having repeated exclusions (78,900 had two or more fixed-period exclusions and the average number of fixed-period exclusions for those that were excluded was 2.2 in 2017/18). The north-east of England saw a jump from 592 fixed period exclusions per 10,000 pupils in the 2016/2017 school year to 934 per 10,000 pupils in 2017/2018 (for reference, London has the lowest rate of fixed-period exclusions at 339 per 10,000 pupils).

Summary

Children for whom mainstream schooling is no longer appropriate (for one of a variety of reasons) can access alternative provision. Doing so offers a way for children to continue their education and have levels of tailored support that would not be available in a mainstream school.

Question 3: What are the signs of stress?

Secondary school is a stressful environment. I describe it like going for a job interview: you're stressed and nervous, and everything you do in the interview is going to matter. That's what a kid's first month is like at school every single day.

(headteacher Janice Allen)

There is no medical definition of stress (it is linked to mental health but it's not a psychiatric diagnosis) and disagreement exists among medical professionals about whether it is the cause of a problem, or the result of it. Stress is a feeling that results from our interpretations of a particular situation.

As we experience and interpret the world around us, our bodies' responses to the feeling of stress can be very useful and wholly desirable (if you think you're about to be eaten by a lion, the stress response that prompts you to run is helpful!). In those moments when we feel threatened, for instance, the heart rate and blood pressure rise, and higher levels of hormones such as cortisol are released (think of this as the body's 'alarm system').

Not all stress responses are detrimental but some are, so it's helpful to separate them in three different categories.

- **Positive stress response:** these responses to the feeling of stress are helpful – they protect us and help us to cope with the environment we face. They may happen, for instance, when a child meets their new teacher for the first time, or just before an important test. The heart rate and stress hormone levels rise a little, but then return to normal again after a short time.
- **Tolerable stress response:** this stronger response may happen, for instance, following a more severe event such as a serious illness or injury, or after the death of a family member. Assuming the stress response is brought under control and the child is supported to adapt to it by adults, the potentially damaging effects of it can be mitigated.
- **Toxic stress response:** this response happens when there is frequent, strong and prolonged exposure to adversity without appropriate adult support. It can occur, for instance, as a result of chronic neglect or abuse. Toxic stress responses can damage the very structures of a child's developing brain and increase their chances of developing mental health problems over their life-course.

In a home or school environment where supportive relationships with adults and other children are strong, stress responses activated in children (by new and challenging situations, an upcoming test or a performance) are more readily managed, brought under control and returned to normal.

WHAT EVERY PARENT SHOULD KNOW ABOUT EDUCATION

THE SIGNS OF STRESS

We can't see stress, but we can see signs of it, and we can acknowledge that the frequency, intensity and duration of it matter. Research summarised and published by Harvard University's Center on the Developing Child (nd) suggests that, with appropriate care, attention and support given by adults, it is possible to mitigate – and, indeed, reverse – the damaging consequences of toxic stress. But first, we need to be able to recognise the signs of it.

Some of the common physical signs of stress to be aware of are:

- headaches;
- low energy;
- stomach upset;
- aches and tense muscles;
- insomnia.

Clearly, there can be lots of causes of these things – everything from dehydration to food poisoning – so it's important to guard against rushing to a conclusion. Nonetheless, stress can affect how a child feels both physically and mentally, and can change their behaviour (the symptoms of stress can also manifest themselves in such ways as a child being withdrawn or being aggressive, or in lateness for lessons and forgetting homework). In schools, leaders, teachers and teaching assistants are on the alert for signs of stress like increased difficulty concentrating and making decisions, appearing overwhelmed and worried or more irritable than usual, and feeling sick (stress can cause physical symptoms such as stomach pain and headaches). And because the indicators of stress are so varied and schools such complex places, teachers and leaders will often use data (classroom behaviour records, attendance records and notes from conversations with children) to look for patterns that raise causes for concern; such work is often useful in identifying low-level problems before they grow.

Ultimately, you know your child better than anyone, so the strong connection and collaboration you build over time with your child's school is one of the ways in which you and they can be more alert and respond to the early signs of potentially damaging stress.

Summary

Stress responses in children and young people can become very problematic when they are frequent, intense and prolonged. Schools – like most places – can be stressful, but through routines and well-ordered environments, teachers and leaders try to reduce stressors, monitor children's well-being and intervene appropriately.

Question 4: What is good mental health?

According to the Mental Health Foundation (MHF, 2020, p 2), good mental health can be described in the following ways:

- *we feel good about ourselves*
- *we can make and keep positive relationships with others*
- *we feel able to manage our feelings rather than feeling overwhelmed by them*
- *we have interests or hobbies that we enjoy*
- *we feel hopeful and positive about the future*

Mental health can be thought of in terms of feeling safe and connected to other people and the wider environment, feeling able to cope, and having a positive state of mind. It's about maintaining mental activity – anything from daily activities in school to having fulfilling relationships with family members and a positive concept of oneself – as well as maintaining the ability and capacity to adapt, change and cope with stress. Schools have well-developed tools and resources for supporting students' mental health, from staff trained to support those with special educational needs and disabilities (the focus of Chapter 9), to access to additional support from professionals such as psychologists.

Yet, even though the evidence around the prevalence of mental health disorders among children and young people is strong, there remains an elephant in the room: many people find talking about mental health uncomfortable to the point of avoidance. Children differ from each other: they hit milestones at different times, they commonly experience behavioural difficulties as they grow, and one in five children experiences some kind of mental health problem. Avoidance of the issue is rarely an effective way of dealing with it.

Many of the mental health problems that adults experience tend to take hold in childhood or early adulthood; attention-deficit hyperactivity disorder (ADHD) commonly begins in children around age five, anxiety in the teen years, and depression in the late teens and early twenties. The combination of a child's genetic predisposition – the DNA they're born with – and experiences of adversity they have in their lives contribute to mental health problems. For both schools and parents, this presents both a challenge (you can't change the DNA of your child) and an opportunity (to focus on making the classroom and home environments the best they possibly can be). But how?

HOW DO SCHOOLS SUPPORT GOOD MENTAL HEALTH?

Headteacher Janice Allen says that positive relationships and dialogue underpin her school's approach to supporting students' mental health. Teachers and leaders do this by creating an environment in which children know and are known by a trusted adult – a class teacher, a form tutor or a mentor. Making a child feel welcome and known in school is a first step in developing a sense of 'relatedness' (a feeling of connection with and mutual support by other people) (Coe et al,

2020), something that itself is part of a larger sense of autonomous motivation that schools seek to promote.

But they go much further than this. Allen – like many senior leaders – fosters dialogue not just about mental health issues, but dialogue in which children express their opinions, and are heard in a safe space that encourages reflection, one that prevents them *shutting down their thoughts*. Honesty and modelling also come into play: adults focus on showing positive responses to challenges they face, especially when things go wrong. They also plan mental health assemblies that are led by children, and have mental health ambassadors and drop-in sessions to support children's mental health. Above all, Allen says, *you encourage empathy in one child towards another child*.

And there is good reason for schools like Allen's to work hard to create open spaces in which the importance of good mental health is recognised and discussed. The majority of mental health problems go untreated; on average, only 30 per cent of those with ill health access the help and support they need (Strathdee, 2015). Left untreated, childhood and adolescent mental health problems can negatively impact adult lives: unemployment, low income and limited social mobility are all associated with untreated mental health problems.

Knowing how to help a child suffering with mental health problems can be daunting, but dialogue and partnership with school can help. If a teacher gets in touch to say that there is an issue with your child that needs attention (be it about mental health or anything else), there can be a danger of feeling that your parenting is being called into question or criticised and, perhaps, that you're even being 'told off' (especially if it's rare for you and your child's teachers to speak directly). But by engaging with school staff regularly, and by maintaining a strong connection with them through parents' meetings and other events, you can collaborate to help both your child *and* yourself.

CULTURAL FACTORS AND MENTAL HEALTH

As we've already seen, up to one in five children experiences mental health problems, and research (summarised from Bor et al, 2014) has begun to question the roles played in these by factors such as:

- worsening income inequality;
- changes in family environment (for instance family conflict, parental mental health problems, and parenting styles that place a lower value on child obedience);
- increased exposure to screen time, the internet and social media;
- pressures associated with school (such as a perceived need to achieve high grades);
- fears around deliberate self-harm, substance misuse and suicide.

But is there really an increase in the incidence of mental health problems among young people in the twenty-first century? Or are changes in the ways we recognise and diagnose conditions making it appear that things are getting worse?

A systematic research review published in the *Australian & New Zealand Journal of Psychiatry* in 2014 by William Bor and colleagues summarised findings from research evidence on changing mental health symptoms among toddlers, children and adolescents. Nineteen high-quality studies from 12 different countries were reviewed, and the results for toddlers and children indicated that there appeared at that time not to be evidence of a *worsening* of mental health problems; indeed, most studies the researchers looked at seemed to suggest that there has been an improvement or at least no change across a range of mental health symptoms for children in these two categories.

Things were different for adolescents, however.

While there seemed to be little change over recent decades in the so-called 'externalising problems' of adolescents (those that come to life in a young person's outward behaviour, such as disruption, hyperactivity and aggression), the evidence on 'internalising problems' (such as withdrawal, anxiety, inhibition and depressed behaviours) points towards an increase in symptoms, especially among girls.

Frustratingly, the evidence is incomplete and unclear, but it does highlight what many parents already sense: a need for caution and vigilance, and a need to reinforce the communication and collaboration with your child's school during their time there.

Summary

Mental health problems affect a lot of children and young people; left untreated, they can adversely affect development into adulthood, so timely intervention is important. Being alert to changes in both externalising and internalising problems is one thing that schools and parents do to look out for and address mental health problems early. Creating and sustaining a strong collaborative relationship with you child's school can help bring potential issues to light early.

Question 5: What can you do to help your child develop good mental health?

As we've already said, being a 'partner' in your child's school experience is an important way in which you can help support their mental health – the strength of the relationship you have with school staff is at the heart of good communication. The research evidence on supporting the development of good mental health offers some 'best bets' (rather than a one-size-fits-all model) that can guide your thinking, and most of what follows in this section won't come as a surprise, nor will the challenge of managing to do it all successfully!

EAT A BALANCED DIET AND EXERCISE REGULARLY

No single food (apart from breastmilk) contains all of the essential nutrients a child's body needs to stay healthy, develop well and function properly. A healthy, balanced diet that provides the right amount of calories (and no more) from unprocessed foods like whole grains, vegetables and fresh fruit can help to stabilise both energy and mood.

Regular physical exercise produces stress-relieving hormones and also helps build the mental skills that enable children to plan, focus attention, remember instructions and deal with situations that induce stress. Exercise can improve a child's abilities to cope with adversity, and to adapt appropriately to it.

SLEEP

To maintain good health, we need to sleep; during the years of childhood development and adolescence, this is incredibly important. The American Academy of Sleep recommends the following amounts of sleep:

Table 8A Recommended sleep

AGE	RECOMMENDED HOURS OF SLEEP WITHIN 24 HOURS
4–12 months	12 to 16 (including naps)
1–2 years	11 to 14 (including naps)
3–5 years	10 to 13 (including naps)
6–12 years	9 to 12
13–18 years	8 to 10

To improve the quality of sleep your child gets, they should avoid consuming drinks that have caffeine in (especially after lunchtime), and evening meals should not be eaten too late, as this can prevent sleep. Having a bedtime routine can help a child understand what to expect before sleep, and limiting the use of electronic devices (TV, mobiles and tablets, for instance) is recommended as part of this routine.

TALK TO TEACHERS AND OTHER PARENTS

Countless other parents at your child's school have faced the challenges of helping their children both develop and maintain good mental health, so being able to talk about your own experiences with them and not think that you have to 'solve' every problem alone can be helpful, even if it may seem daunting at first.

Schools can't solve every problem experienced by every child, but they often have strong links to external youth services, community groups and mental health support organisations. Talk to your child's teachers to see what resources might be available to learn more about and support healthy mental development.

TAKE CARE OF YOURSELF

To take care of those around you, you need first to take care of yourself. Paying attention to the development of your own physical and emotional health can help you handle the challenges that come with supporting a child experiencing mental health problems and illness. Above all, acknowledge that, as headteacher Janice Allen puts it, *'parenting is really hard and no matter what you do at certain points, it's going to go wrong'.*

Summary

You can help your child to be 'school ready' by providing a safe home and nutritious food, and by encouraging sleep and exercise – none of this will be news to most parents. In addition, taking care of your own physical and mental health has to be a priority.

Conclusion

Teachers and school leaders are not psychologists or counsellors but they do have access to them; we must be careful not to expect the world of them, or to elevate what they are able to do with a child's education beyond the realms of reality. The role of a teacher is demanding enough without adding the expectation of being an expert in every aspect of child development, such as stress and mental health: it would be crazy to think that someone with no medical training would diagnose a case of pancreatic cancer, and it's similarly nonsensical to expect a non-specialist to diagnose mental health problems.

When there are concerns about a child experiencing prolonged or heightened stress on a regular basis, pastoral care teams in schools may request the services of a mental health professional such as an educational psychologist. Psychologists have special training to help people identify issues and develop ways of resolving and coping with feelings that may overwhelm them.

❖ What to talk about on parents' evening

Without having a **clear model** of the behaviours you want your child to develop, repeatedly *correcting* children – rather than describing, modelling and supporting the development of the desired behaviour – becomes increasingly likely. Tom Bennett points out that schools manage behaviour effectively when they define what is meant by '*good* behaviour' and provide clear models of it. You could ask your child's teacher:

- What does 'good' behaviour mean in my child's class, and how is it modelled?

- What school and classroom routines should I know about and what can I do to reinforce these at home?

- What steps are taken when a child behaves inappropriately in school?

Finding out about your child's school's **approach to monitoring and managing stress** and mental health issues may also be helpful, so here are some questions that might get the conversation started with teachers and school leaders.

- How does the school promote good mental health?

- Who should I talk to in school if I have a concern about my child's mental health?

further reading

» One great starting point for further reading is the website www.teenmentalhealth.org/. It's a resource for parents and educators with enormously useful information on what schools and parents can do to help support good mental health.

» You can also find out more about mental health and how you can support your child by visiting www.mentalhealth.org.uk/.

» Additionally Sarah-Jayne Blakemore's award-winning *Inventing Ourselves: The Secret Life of the Teenage Brain* (2018) is a fascinating and very readable explanation of adolescence. Highly recommended if you want to take a peek inside the inner workings of the developing brain.

Bibliography

Bennett, T (2017) *Creating a Culture: How School Leaders Can Optimise Behaviour*. [online] Available at: https://assets.publishing.service.gov.uk/government/uploads/system/uploads/attachment_data/file/602487/Tom_Bennett_Independent_Review_of_Behaviour_in_Schools.pdf (accessed 15 February 2021).

Blakemore, S-J (2018) *Inventing Ourselves: The Secret Life of the Teenage Brain*. Harmondsworth: Penguin.

Bor, W, Dean, A J, Najman, J and Hayatbakhsh, R (2014) Are Child and Adolescent Mental Health Problems Increasing in the 21st Century? A Systematic Review. *Australian & New Zealand Journal of Psychiatry*, 48(7): 606–16.

Coe, R, Raunch, C J, Kime, S and Singleton, D (2020) *The Great Teaching Toolkit: Evidence Review*. [online] Available at: www.greatteaching.com (accessed 15 February 2021).

Harvard University's Center on the Developing Child (nd) A Guide to Toxic Stress. [online] Available at: https://developingchild.harvard.edu/guide/a-guide-to-toxic-stress/ (accessed 15 April 2021).

MHF (2020) Mental Health Foundation. [online] Available at: www.mentalhealth.org.uk/sites/default/files/mental-health-schools-make-it-count-pupils-guide.pdf (accessed 15 February 2021).

Morrison Gutman, L and Vorhaus, J (2012) *The Impact of Pupil Behaviour and Wellbeing on Educational Outcomes*. London: Institute of Education, University of London.

Ofsted (2014) *Below the Radar: Low-Level Disruption in the Country's Classrooms*. [online] Available at: https://assets.publishing.service.gov.uk/government/uploads/system/uploads/attachment_data/file/379249/Below_20the_20radar_20-_20low-level_20disruption_20in_20the_20country_E2_80_99s_20classrooms.pdf (accessed 15 February 2021).

Skipp, A and Hopwood, V (2017) *Case Studies of Behaviour Management Practices in Schools Rated Outstanding*. [online] Available at: https://assets.publishing.service.gov.uk/government/uploads/system/uploads/attachment_data/file/602506/Behaviour_Management_Case_Studies_Report.pdf (accessed 15 February 2021).

Spielman, A (2019) HMCI Commentary: Managing Behaviour Research. [online] Available at: www.gov.uk/government/speeches/research-commentary-managing-behaviour (accessed 15 February 2021).

Strathdee, G (2015) A Defining Moment in Mental Health Care. [online] Available at: www.england.nhs.uk/blog/geraldine-strathdee-8/ (accessed 15 February 2021).

WHO (2017) Depression and Other Common Mental Disorders: Global Health Estimates. [online] Available at: https://apps.who.int/iris/bitstream/handle/10665/254610/WHO-MSD-MER-2017.2-eng.pdf;jsessionid=FE1D043AFB250FD6C377CB4AC69951B0?sequence=1 (accessed 15 February 2021).

9. DYSLEXIA, DYSPRAXIA AND OTHER SPECIFIC LEARNING DISABILITIES

Key information

When a child is diagnosed as having a learning problem it demands the highest level of collaboration and understanding between parents and schools. It can also prompt a shift in how the child is viewed, both by the school and by themselves, which can have a profound impact on confidence and progress. Whether this impact is positive or negative depends upon how the issue is treated. The research suggests that good support for specific learning disabilities goes beyond labels and medical diagnosis, and looks at the child's individual emotional and learning needs.

- Beware a one-size-fits-all approach to dealing with a diagnosis. Specific learning disabilities are not straightforward medical conditions with established treatments, but complex conditions that often manifest in very individual ways.
- Focus on understanding your child's needs rather than worrying about the label they have been given. Provide emotional support as well as assistance with their learning.
- The most important support in the school is still the child's teacher. Work with them to understand and meet the individual needs of your child.

The most common questions about specific learning disabilities

In this chapter we explore the following questions.

1. What are the most common specific learning disabilities?
2. Is the number of students with SEND diagnoses increasing?
3. If my child is diagnosed with a specific learning disability, are the SENDCo and the classroom teaching assistants now responsible for my child's learning?
4. How well do we understand specific learning disabilities?
5. Does the environment affect specific learning disabilities?
6. What is the best way to teach a child with a learning disability?

Question 1: What are the most common specific learning disabilities?

To do the broad spectrum of special educational issues justice would take a lot more than a single chapter, so this chapter only looks at specific learning disabilities such as dyslexia, dyspraxia and ADHD, rather than the full spectrum of medical conditions that can impact a child's learning. Table 9A summarises the most common specific learning disabilities.

Table 9A Common specific learning disabilities

CONDITION	WHAT IS IT?	HOW COMMON IT IS?
Dyslexia	A term used to describe a range of reading and language processing disabilities, but often also linked to other conditions such as Irlen Syndrome or dyspraxia.	Estimates vary, but it is generally believed that 10 per cent of the population is partially dyslexic, with 4 per cent seriously dyslexic (NHS, 2018).
Dyspraxia/ Developmental Co-ordination Disorder (DCD)	A term used to describe a wide range of co-ordination and motor skill deficiencies. It was originally termed 'clumsy child syndrome'.	An estimated 5 per cent of the population are dyspraxic (Zwicker et al, 2018).
Dyscalculia	A specific impairment in a child's maths and numeracy skills, similar to the impairment dyslexia sufferers have with reading.	Estimates vary from 4 per cent to 7 per cent (Butterworth, 2008).
ADHD	A persistent inability to pay attention, combined with physical restlessness and impulsivity, that cannot be easily explained as the result of environmental factors.	ADHD occurs in about 5 per cent of children and about 2.5 per cent of adults (American Psychiatric Association, 2013).

The world of special educational needs is also rich with acronyms and euphemisms that can make it seem a little hard to understand initially. Table 9B provides a quick glossary of the most common terms you will encounter.

Table 9B Table of common special educational needs terms

SEND	*Special Educational Needs and Disability.* An umbrella term used to describe any personal needs that might act as a barrier to learning in some way. The categories of SEND issues includes: - communication and social interaction needs; - cognition and learning needs; - social, emotional, personal and mental health needs; - sensory and physical needs.
Specific learning disabilities	A specific cognitive disability that impairs the learning process, particularly by making it difficult to process information or communicate. Most commonly, it means conditions like dyslexia, dyspraxia or ADHD. Specific learning disabilities are a specific category within the wider SEND spectrum. For example, depression might constitute a special educational need as it affects your ability to learn normally, but it is not a specific learning disability in the same way that dyslexia is.
SENDCo	*Special Educational Needs Co-ordinator* (usually referred to by the acronym SENDCo). This is a member of staff with specialist training in special educational needs, and who is responsible for overseeing the SEND provision in that school. These specialists have additional academic qualifications and may do a lot of the initial diagnosis of specific learning disabilities themselves then make the referrals to educational psychologists for formal diagnosis.
EHCP (sometimes EHC)	An *Education, Health and Care Plan.* In more complex or serious cases, the school or the parents may refer a student for an EHC assessment which the local education authority will assess and draw up and then submit to the school and the parents for approval.

Summary

There is a lot of jargon around special educational needs, but if you learn the few key terms and ideas you should be able to navigate through the information available relatively easily. In particular, it is useful to understand the distinction between specific learning disabilities such as dyslexia and dyspraxia, and the wider spectrum of disability.

Question 2: Is the number of students with SEND diagnoses increasing?

This is a very controversial question within education. Progressive narratives around education tend to assume that numbers are increasing, and that this must be due to better diagnosis and increased sensitivity to student needs. However, others have expressed concern about the numbers of students who are getting diagnosed, arguing that funding incentives are leading to over-diagnosis and unnecessary labelling of students. The available data doesn't prove either of these scenarios to be accurate. Government data shows that numbers of SEND diagnoses are indeed increasing, but slowly, and they are overall down from a high of 21.1 per cent in 2010 to 14.9 per cent today.

More noticeable has been the increases in EHC plans for more severe specific learning disabilities, which has been slowly but steadily increasing over the past few years to nearly 354,000 in 2019, up from 235,980 in 2015.

Summary

The numbers of SEND diagnoses is increasing, but they are not at an all-time high. In contrast, the numbers of students receiving EHC plans is the highest it has ever been, although increase has been steady. It is not possible to tell from the available evidence whether either of these rises are due to improvements in diagnosis or the incentivisation of schools to diagnose students.

Question 3: If my child is diagnosed with a specific learning disability, are the SENDCo and the classroom teaching assistants now responsible for my child's learning?

For a child with a specific learning disability, the most important person in the school is not the SENDCo but the child's teacher. Once a child is diagnosed, some parents worry that they have now shifted to some separate but parallel educational system within the school that is led by the SENDCo, but this is not the case.

The SENDCo's role is meant to be overseeing your child's education and acting as advocate for their needs, although the exact role of the SENDCo will vary significantly from school to school. For example, the current *SEND Code of Practice* states that SENDCos should be part of the school leadership team (DfE and DoH, 2015, p 108) but in some schools the role may be much more marginal. Whatever role the SENDCo plays, the classroom teacher is ultimately going to be responsible for teaching your child. The wider school community may also play a role (through additional support classes, SENDCo interventions and teaching assistants), but the main relationship to cultivate is that you have with their teacher.

It is a similar story with classroom teaching assistants. If you have never encountered classroom assistants before, these are adults who take part in lessons and assist the teacher to deliver classes. As any teacher will tell you, these are often the unsung heroes of the classroom, although their use is sometimes controversial. As their use has increased alongside the increase in numbers of SEND students (Santry, 2018), it is tempting to make the assumption that their role in classrooms is to teach struggling students while the teacher gets on with teaching the rest of the class. However, in a review of the research evidence on classroom teaching assistants, the Education Endowment Foundation says that *'TAs should not be used as an informal teaching resource for low attaining pupils'* (Sharples et al, 2016, p 10) and that classroom assistants are best deployed delivering high-quality group and one-to-one support for struggling pupils. This means that while a classroom assistant may well help a student with special educational needs as part of their role, this should only be in support of the regular teaching that the child has received from the teacher, and must be planned and organised in the first instance by the teacher so as to be effective. If a child is struggling, why should they be the person least likely to get one-to-one attention from the teacher?

Summary

While the SENDCo is an important person to have a relationship with, it is the classroom teacher who is primarily responsible for your child's learning. Classroom teaching assistants are also not there to replace the regular teacher, they are there to help the teacher in a range of support issues. As such they may help support SEND learners by allowing the teacher time to give additional support to SEND students, or by helping reinforce regular learning through targeted small-group support.

Question 4: How well do we understand specific learning disabilities?

The more you read about common specific learning disabilities, the more you come to a single conclusion: treat students as individuals, not as labels. Good schools and teachers understand that specific learning disabilities aren't simple tick-box medical conditions that are easy to diagnose and cure. Instead the research paints a complex picture that can often become oversimplified in the rush to support a child.

WE DON'T FULLY UNDERSTAND THE UNDERLYING CAUSES OF MOST SPECIFIC LEARNING DISABILITIES

There is no doubt that the recent advances in genetics and neurological research have begun to paint a more detailed picture of the causes of specific learning disabilities, and we can have some confidence these gaps are starting to be filled in. But the more we understand about the impact of genes, the less it looks like there is a simple genetic or environmental cause for each one. Certainly, most specific learning disabilities are inherited to some extent, but the exact impact of genetics is still not fully understood. ADHD has '*no single risk factor*' (Thapar et al, 2013, p 3) and appears to be a product of (as yet) unmeasurable genetic and environmental factors. DCD/dyspraxia is also poorly understood on a genetic and neurological level (Leonard et al, 2015), although recent research is starting to change this.

The lack of clarity on the origins of specific learning disabilities makes it difficult to have clear therapies for them. The fact they are largely genetic also means that there is no 'cure' as such. All of which reinforces the need for schools and parents to take a needs-based approach.

MANY SPECIFIC LEARNING DISABILITIES ARE DIFFICULT TO DEFINE AND SOME MAY NOT ACTUALLY BE DEFINABLE CONDITIONS AT ALL

Even when we have a lot of research into a condition, it doesn't necessarily lead to more clarity for parents and teachers. For example, dyslexia is probably the most intensely researched of all the specific learning disabilities (alongside ADHD), but instead of revealing a simple basis to the condition, these findings have caused some psychologists to doubt whether we should even use the term 'dyslexic' at all (Elliott and Grigorenko, 2014). There doesn't seem to be a single dysfunction in cognition or the brain that we can point to as the cause, and we haven't found a simple genetic basis for the condition either. In fact, the more we research dyslexia, the more it looks like a clutch of different literacy disabilities with overlapping symptoms. That's not in any way to suggest that children with dyslexia are imagining their difficulties, only that their problems are diverse in origin and need to be dealt with on a person-by-person basis.

Similar definitional issues can be found in a commonly-diagnosed condition called Meares-Irlen syndrome (usually referred to as just Irlen syndrome) which supposedly leads to children experiencing 'visual stress' with images jumping around and making it very hard to read. Children diagnosed with this syndrome are given visual adjustments to help them read in the form of coloured visual overlays, special glasses (called Irlen lenses) or coloured paper. Despite the syndrome being a relatively orthodox medical position in the recent past, the latest analysis of the research questions both the efficacy of the treatment and even the existence of the condition itself, arguing the whole idea is extrapolated from quite poor-quality research (Miyasaka et al, 2019). In addition, there is very little evidence for the effectiveness of popular methods for supporting these students such as coloured paper, visual overlays and glasses with special lenses. This is not to say that there is no such thing as visual stress, or that it is pointless to help students who experience it, but it shows how quickly a whole condition and set of seemingly valid treatments can emerge around questionable evidence.

These definitional issues multiply when you realise that specific learning disabilities rarely manifest in isolation and there is often an overlap between different conditions. Large numbers of children with one learning disability often have another. These overlaps make diagnosis more difficult as specific learning disabilities often share symptoms and it also makes it difficult to know exactly which condition is causing which behavioural issue, complicating treatment choices. If you aren't sure what is causing a child to exhibit certain symptoms, picking the wrong therapy, support or medical intervention may actually be harmful.

Summary

Diagnoses for common SEND issues are not simple medical diagnoses that require a clear treatment. Appropriately supporting a child with SEND requires listening to individual needs and tailoring support to those needs, rather than a one-size-fits-all approach.

Question 5: Does the environment affect specific learning disabilities?

Despite the largely genetic origins of common specific learning disabilities, their actual impact upon the child is largely determined by their emotional and cultural environment. Parents and schools have a massive role to play in helping children to adapt and thrive by creating the right environment.

Children with specific learning disabilities often experience issues with self-esteem and self-confidence (Humphrey and Mullins, 2002; Shaw-Zirt et al, 2005). These issues can then act as a feedback loop, causing a child to spiral downwards when they may need to work harder than their peers. Similarly, those behaviours that eventually lead to a diagnosis aren't distinct from the condition itself. For example, a child may be acting out or refusing to work because of an undiagnosed condition, but this doesn't mean that the behaviour itself shouldn't be addressed as well. Both the behaviour and the learning may need to be supported to get the child back to success.

Summary

When trying to support a child with a learning disability, attention and care must also be paid to the environmental and emotional dimensions of their condition.

Question 6: What is the best way to teach a child with a learning disability?

Historically, the central debate around teaching a child with a learning disability has been whether their education should be inclusive or exclusive. Should SEND kids be part of regular education? Or are they better off being taught in environments tailored to their needs? In recent times, opinion has coalesced around the notion of inclusion – wherever possible children should be educated with their peers – but do they actually need to be taught differently in the classroom? Unless they have a severe condition, the principle of inclusion applies to the learning process as well. Wherever possible, children with specific learning disabilities need to access the same knowledge and skills as their peers, they just have additional barriers in their way. That said, there are some strategies that research has shown to be particularly effective for specific learning disabilities. The most common ones are summarised in Table 9C.

Table 9C Common treatments of specific learning disabilities

CONDITION	COMMON TREATMENTS AND THERAPIES
Dyslexia	Studies of common dyslexia interventions have shown how directly teaching core reading and writing skills through systematic, explicit instruction can significantly improve the skills of dyslexic children. Similarly, teaching children explicit strategies for writing that focus on problem-solving, planning, and self-regulation also seem to be effective (Reid, 2019). In practice this means techniques such as: - Additional time to think and process. - Intense support in learning the phonetic and symbolic structures of English. - Regular assessment focusing on their specific dyslexic needs. - Helping children to understand their learning process and providing strategies to cope with their challenges. - More heavily scaffolding language that is used in the classroom, whether written or oral.
Dyspraxia/ DCD	Dyspraxia is a lifelong condition without a cure, but there are some perceptual, cognitive (Thornton et al, 2016) and motor-training therapies (Smits-Eldsman et al, 2013) that have been found to support development and reduce the impact of DCD. In most cases a child with severe DCD will work with a therapist to improve their ability to deal with specific tasks or to work on general co-ordination and motor skills.

CONDITION	COMMON TREATMENTS AND THERAPIES
Dyscalculia	The most effective intervention is explicit instruction in strategies that target the specific mathematical deficits of students with dyscalculia (Haberstroh and Schulte-Körne, 2019). In practice this means: • Focusing on core number skills in younger students. • Using assessment to diagnose the precise issues the sufferer experiences. • Targeting these challenges with additional tuition and assessment. • Encouraging specialised practice to strengthen areas of academic weakness.
ADHD	Medication is common, and its use has been increasing over time (Renoux et al, 2016), but it remains controversial and some medical professionals have expressed concern at the high rates of diagnosis and prescriptions. Most effective drug combinations use stimulants in some form. Non-stimulant options are available, but these have been found to be less effective. Evidence for the effectiveness of drug interventions remains good, however, although the National Collaborating Centre for Mental Health says *'uncertainty still surrounds the quality of evidence and the balance of risks and benefits of long-term drug treatment for ADHD in children and young people'* (2009, p 210). Other therapies that are available include relaxation and breathing techniques and cognitive behavioural therapy, but neither of these have the same evidence of impact as the medications that are available.

AVOIDING BOGUS TREATMENTS

It's worth noting that there is a depressing number of 'alternative' therapies out there for all these conditions, none of which have a solid evidence base for their efficacy. These treatments are best avoided, and any anecdotal benefits they may proclaim are usually the result of the placebo effect or the natural improvements in some conditions over time. While some of these are truly outlandish and obviously wacky (crystal healing and aromatherapy, anyone?), there are others that can look much more scientific and may even market themselves as such. The most common of these are listed in Table 9D.

Table 9D Common alternative therapies for learning disorders

CONDITION	COMMON ALTERNATIVE THERAPIES
Dyslexia	Auditory therapies, massage therapies, nutritional therapies, movement-based therapies, homeopathy.
Dyspraxia/DCD	Nutritional and diet therapies, neuro-developmental therapy, sound therapy, homeopathy.
Dyscalculia	Nutritional and diet therapies, homeopathy, multisensory instruction.
ADHD	Nutritional and diet therapies, neuro-developmental therapy, homeopathy, neurofeedback.*

* Neurofeedback is a therapy involving using live brain feedback to help children train their brains – this is actually being seriously scientifically explored but it is extremely time-consuming, and results have been mixed. It is included here because some unscrupulous therapists have adopted the language around it to promote unrelated alternative therapies.

Before you begin any treatment, check its validity with a qualified medical expert, and it is also worth remembering these warning signs of likely bogus therapies:

- claims that they are evidence-based, but do not link to any actual research papers;
- makes implausible claims about effectiveness;
- promoted by people who mention their qualifications a lot but don't make it clear what those qualifications are in or have qualifications that prove dubious upon investigation;
- uses scientific-sounding words in a vague fashion;
- talks down the medical profession or presents therapy as an alternative to traditional medical routes.

Summary

Children with a specific learning disability do not need to learn in a completely unique way, but instead need to have the regular learning process tailored to meet their needs. Teachers can identify these needs by listening carefully to parents and children, and closely monitoring their progress. For many common specific learning disabilities, the most powerful solutions involve better instruction and more intensive versions of existing learning strategies. Beware bogus therapies that seem to offer easy solutions. In most cases, there are no shortcuts when it comes to helping SEND students.

Margaret Mulholland is a SEND and inclusion specialist at the Association of School and College Leaders.

In your opinion, what does excellent SEND provision look like?

When it is built into the teaching and learning of the school and not bolted on. When it is kept simple and focused on positive outcomes for young people with SEND. When the leadership of the school is involved in the discussion. When each young person is 'known and understood' by all teachers. Knowledge of his or her cognitive capacity allows tailoring of the curriculum and teaching to play to strengths and navigate any barriers.

In your experience, what are the most common misconceptions that parents have about the role of a SENDCo?

The SENDCo plays an important role in navigating the connections between needs and provision. However, the delivery is actually the job of the teachers in the classroom. Understanding the actual influence the SENDCo has is important, which can depend on their seniority in the school. Initial sympathy, which parents are often grateful for, needs to translate to long-term empathy and quality provision. IPSEA (Independent Provider of Special Education Advice) offers great legal training for parents – well worth doing.

What are the most important things for parents of a child with a SEND diagnosis to understand?

First, that the diagnosis doesn't define who they are or what their young person is capable of. A diagnosis is really a place for the teacher to start, not to finish. We tend to focus on immediate needs in the school context; parents need to think long-term as well as short-term. What will the child's life be like, for example, in ten or 15 years' time? And set expectations from the beginning. I would add a cautious note about the additional cost – both financial and emotional – on the family.

In your opinion, how useful are terms like 'dyslexic' or 'ADHD' for helping to understand a child's support needs?

These terms are useful as a place to start. A specific and detailed educational or clinical psychologist's report that supports the diagnosis can be more useful to translate this into classroom strategies that fit the particular profile of the child.

Where can parents find high-quality information about SEND issues and individual conditions?

__Special Needs Jungle__ is the Mumsnet equivalent for SEND. Find a charitable organisation that represents the things you find important. The __SEND Code of Practice__ is also a useful resource, more from understanding what expectations of support there are.

What are useful things a parent can do to help a school understand their child's needs?

Communicate regularly and positively (don't leave it to the annual review process) and set expectations and targets that are as simple as possible to understand. Pitch your communications low – assume they know very little, as teachers are busy and need your help to recognise the nuance of the need for your child. Suggest your child has a responsibility in the class or year group, whether primary or secondary. Think about what will give them a sense of confident responsibility, something they can achieve. Some children with SEND communicate more confidently with adults, so starting the day helping in the school office, delivering registers, fruit or whatever can provide a positive hook to start the day.

If parents are unsatisfied with the support their child is receiving what do you think is the most effective way to tackle it?

Don't let it slip by without raising it with the teacher, the SENDCo and the escalation process in the school (usually head of year, then headteacher). Keep a daily diary and be diligent with writing down what is happening and what you are happy with/dissatisfied with. Look for positive steps forward as well as the challenges. Most schools will work hard to do the right thing for the child, but the balancing of resources and dedicated support is a reality. Don't accept the statement 'there are 29 other children in the class I need to think about'; every good teacher should be able to support all the children, including yours, in every class.

Conclusion

Specific learning disabilities like dyslexia and dyscalculia are not simple medical conditions with prescribed cures, although there may be a medical or therapeutic dimension to how these children are supported. Teachers and parents should both focus on understanding and meeting the individual needs of the student, and focus on removing the obstacles to learning, instead of treating children with specific learning disabilities as being incapable of learning normally.

❖ What to talk about on parents' evening

- **The SENDCo role.** Ask about the role the SENDCo plays in the school. Where does the SENDCo fit in the management structure? What responsibilities do they have?

- **Classroom assistants.** How are they used? Do they do any work with kids with specific learning disabilities? If so, how do they work?

- **Helping support your child.** Perhaps the most powerful thing you can ask is: 'What do you need to know about my child to help you teach them?' You're the expert on them and probably understand their needs better than anyone. Provide what information you can and try to agree what you should be doing to help them at home.

further reading

There is a lot of poor-quality SEND advice out there and a lack of high-quality, trustworthy sources of information. However, the following websites and publications may be of some use if you are looking for effective further reading on evidence-informed approaches to SEND:

» A good starting point for parents of kids who have been diagnosed with SEN is the Special Needs Jungle (www.specialneedsjungle.com/). Like all user-contributed sites, you should be careful not to take everything on there at face value and try to triangulate information with other reputable sources.

» Another useful site for people is the Independent Provider of Special Education Advice (www.ipsea.org.uk/), although its remit is less to do with teaching itself, and more to do with navigating the legal frameworks used for SEN support.

» *The researchED Guide to Special Educational Needs* (Wespieser, 2020) is an excellent book for teachers, which is useful for parents too. It is written by many of the foremost names in evidence-informed education and contains a lot of good advice.

Bibliography

American Psychiatric Association (2013) *Diagnostic and Statistical Manual of Mental Disorders (DSM-5)*. Arlington, VA: American Psychiatric Association.

Butterworth, B (2008) Developmental Dyscalculia. In Reed, J and Warner-Rogers, C (eds) *Child Neuropsychology: Concepts, Theory, and Practice* (pp 357-74). New Jersey: Wiley-Blackwell.

DfE and DoH (2015) *Special Educational Needs and Disability Code of Practice: 0 to 25 Years*. [online] Available at: http://assets.publishing.service.gov.uk/government/uploads/system/uploads/attachment_data/file/398815/SEND_Code_of_Practice_January_2015.pdf (accessed 15 February 2021).

Elliott, J G and Grigorenko, E L (2014) *The Dyslexia Debate*. Cambridge: Cambridge University Press.

Haberstroh, S and Schulte-Körne, G (2019) The Diagnosis and Treatment of Dyscalculia. *Deutsches Ärzteblatt International*, 116: 107.

Humphrey, N and Mullins, P M (2002) Self-Concept and Self-Esteem in Developmental Dyslexia. *Journal of Research in Special Educational Needs*, 2(2).

Leonard, H C, Bernardi, M, Hill, E L and Henry, L A (2015) Executive Functioning, Motor Difficulties, and Developmental Coordination Disorder. *Developmental Neuropsychology*, 40: 201-15.

Miyasaka, J D S, Vieira, R V G, Novalo-Goto, E S, Montagna, E and Wajnsztejn, R (2019) Irlen Syndrome: Systematic Review and Level of Evidence Analysis. *Arquivos de Neuro-Psiquiatria*, 77: 194–207.

National Collaborating Centre for Mental Health (2009) *Attention Deficit Hyperactivity Disorder: Diagnosis and Management of ADHD in Children, Young People and Adults*. London: British Psychological Society.

NHS (2018) Dyslexia: Symptoms. [online] Available at: www.nhs.uk/conditions/dyslexia/symptoms/ (accessed 15 February 2021).

Reid, G (2019) *Dyslexia and Inclusion*, 3rd edition. New York: Routledge.

Renoux, C, Shin, J-Y, Dell'Aniello, S, Fergusson, E and Suissa, S (2016) Prescribing Trends of Attention-Deficit Hyperactivity Disorder (ADHD) Medications in UK Primary Care, 1995–2015. *British Journal of Clinical Pharmacology*, 82: 858–68.

Santry, C (2018) Exclusive: Army of Teaching Assistants Continued to Expand Even as Funding Squeeze Began. *Times Educational Supplement*. [online] Available at: www.tes.com/news/exclusive-army-teaching-assistants-continued-expand-even-funding-squeeze-began (accessed 15 February 2021).

Sharples, J, Blatchford, P and Webster, R (2016) *Making Best Use of Teaching Assistants*. London: Education Endowment Foundation.

Shaw-Zirt, B, Popali-Lehane, L, Chaplin, W and Bergman, A (2005) Adjustment, Social Skills, and Self-Esteem in College Students with Symptoms of ADHD. *Journal of Attention Disorders*, 8: 109–20.

Smits-Eldsman, B, Blank, R, Van Der Kay, A-C, Mosterd Van De Meijs, R, Vlugut Van Den Brand, E, Polatajko, H J and Wilson, P H (2013) Efficacy of Interventions to Improve Motor Performance in Children with Developmental Coordination Disorder: A Combined Systematic Review and Meta-Analysis. *Developmental Medicine & Child Neurology*, 55: 229–37.

Thapar, A, Cooper, M, Eyre, O and Langley, K (2013) Practitioner Review: What Have We Learnt about the Causes of ADHD? *Journal of Child Psychology and Psychiatry*, 54: 3–16.

Thornton, A, Licari, M, Reid, S, Armstrong, J, Fallows, R and Elliott, C (2016) Cognitive Orientation to (Daily) Occupational Performance Intervention Leads to Improvements in Impairments, Activity and Participation in Children with Developmental Coordination Disorder. *Disability and Rehabilitation*, 38: 979–86.

Wespieser, K (ed) (2020) *The researchED Guide to Special Educational Needs: An Evidence-Informed Guide for Teachers*. Melton, Woodbridge: John Catt Educational Ltd.

Zwicker, J G, Suto, M, Harris, S R, Vlasakova, N and Missiuna, C (2018) Developmental Coordination Disorder is More than a Motor Problem: Children Describe the Impact of Daily Struggles on their Quality of Life. *British Journal of Occupational Therapy*, 81: 65–73.

10. HOW TO USE THE KNOWLEDGE IN THIS BOOK

What does a supportive parent do on a day-to-day basis?

We hope that you can support your child's education even more if you put into practice what you have learnt in this book, and if you also approach your relationship with school in a collaborative way. Table 10A outlines some good habits to adopt.

Table 10A Habits of supportive parents

HABITS	EXAMPLES
1. Establish a routine	The effort of studying is made easier by regular patterns of work and rest. • Set aside clear working hours and play hours. • Regulate the alternatives to working, for example, screen time. • Make sure they have a regular sleep routine. • Encourage them to complete all their work before stopping so that it doesn't become a mental burden. • Share their working time. For example, have a *family work time* where you work alongside them, modelling effort and concentration for them to see.
2. Make learning part of everyday activity	Particularly for younger children, every experience is a learning opportunity. • Read and experience culture together as a family. • Highlight new vocabulary and new concepts, and ask questions about them.
3. Revisit learning and encourage practice	The home can be a great place to extend and reinforce learning that is taking place at school. • Encourage practice even beyond what the teacher may require – if a child wants to get better at something give them opportunities to improve through practice. • Ask them about what they are learning. Get them to summarise and reflect on what they have learnt.
4. Treat assessment as an opportunity for learning	While you should be sensitive to exam stress and badly managed assessment in school, don't contribute to exam stress at home. • Don't fixate on grades. They rarely capture reality. Show excitement and enthusiasm for assessment. Treat them as games to be enjoyed or opportunities for practice. • Focus any discussion on how to improve rather than the grade or mark they have achieved. Praise effort more than success.

→

Table 10A (Cont.)

5. Build strong relationships with your child's teacher and school	Use the advice in this book to build a strong, collaborative relationship with your teacher. • Ask positive questions. • Discuss the curriculum and learning itself.
6. Have high expectations but be sensitive to your child's needs	It will always be a tricky balancing act for parents to weigh their child's individual needs against their own expectations, but talk to your children about their goals, and about their futures, as well as their challenges and struggles.

How should I manage my relationship with the school?

Like any relationship, the link between the parent and the school will vary depending upon the nature of the school and the personality of the parent. But there are reasonable expectations you should have of each other and unspoken rules that everyone should follow. For example, it is reasonable for the school to expect you, as a parent, to do the following.

- **Follow the processes of the school and respect the leadership structure.** Schools usually have both informal and formal channels through which to communicate with parents. Most schools appreciate it when minor issues are raised informally, and the complaints procedure is reserved for genuine disagreement or dissatisfaction. Similarly, it can be counterproductive to try and circumvent teachers and middle leaders by going straight to the headteacher as it can frame any criticism as a reputational issue rather than an individual issue.
- **Don't publicly criticise the school.** Even if you find yourself at odds with those of the school, angry posts on local Facebook groups or negative reviews on Google are quick ways to back the school into a corner and make it difficult to find a resolution. Similarly, taking the story to the local press will probably cause trust to break down completely. Schools are rarely allowed to present their own side of the story when the press run stories about them and hurting a school's reputation may hurt your child's education in the long run as it may have a negative impact on the school's standing within the community.

While teachers can expect these things of parents, parents can expect certain behaviours from schools. It is reasonable for you to expect the school to do the following.

- **Communicate clearly and directly with you.** Schools should be honest about what is going on in their classrooms, even if their interpretation of events may differ from your own, and they should always communicate with you themselves, not through intermediaries.

- **Follow up all concerns quickly and effectively.** When issues are raised, schools should reply to emails and phone calls within a day or so, although it is always worth remembering that schoolteachers have incredibly busy jobs.
- **Follow its own processes in good faith.** The school's internal processes should be compliant with all relevant legislation and be overseen by governors. The schools should always follow these processes wherever possible.

HOW TO TALK TO A SCHOOL WHEN YOU HAVE AN ISSUE

While knowledgeable and collaborative parents usually have positive interactions with schools, there will always be occasions where you and the school may disagree about the decisions being made for your child. When this happens, we recommend the following principles for achieving a successful resolution.

Speak directly to the relevant people with a view to finding a resolution

Too often, the problems experienced arise from miscommunication or misunderstanding. A direct email or a phone call to the relevant person can go a long way towards framing the conversation in the right way and getting people to understand your concerns.

Similarly, demanding action or threatening the school is rarely positive. It puts schools and teachers on the defensive and is likely to initiate a formal complaints procedure that can stifle positive action. Unless you think the school's response is actively dangerous, you are usually better starting by assuming good intentions on the part of the school.

Ask questions and try to appreciate the individual context of any decision

Teachers make hundreds of decisions every day in difficult contexts which parents might not fully be aware of. What may seem problematic when viewed in isolation may be an effective compromise when viewed in the context of time pressures, the expectations of senior leadership, the wider school culture and the needs of other students. If you try to understand these contextual factors then you may better understand the school's choices and it should lead to a productive discussion. To that end, try to phrase issues as questions, not as statements. For example:

DON'T SAY	DO SAY
There's too much homework being given out.	Can you help me understand why students are being given this amount of homework? It seems excessive to me.
A lot of geography homework you give out is completely pointless.	What was the goal of asking students to make a model of a volcano for their geography homework?

Challenge practice, not individuals

Teachers are people too, with their own feeling and foibles. It is usually sensible to take the emotion out of any discussion by focusing on the teaching practice itself, not the individual teachers and their decisions. For example:

DON'T SAY	DO SAY
I don't think Mr Smith is doing enough retrieval practice.	My daughter is struggling to remember things in her history lessons, and I'm worried she's not doing enough retrieval practice in class.
You obviously believe in the discredited ideas of learning styles and you have labelled my child a kinaesthetic learner. This could really damage their education.	My child is being told she's a kinaesthetic learner. As I understand it, there isn't much evidence that using learning styles are real.

Give yourself and the teacher time to reflect

It may be that it is possible to quickly find a way forward, particularly if the teacher is able to reassure you that they are making suitable choices for your child. But if the situation is not easily resolved, it may be sensible to ask them for additional time for everyone to reflect. The teacher (or senior leader) may need to consult other people, particularly if what you are asking about is linked to whole-school policy. Agree a time to revisit the conversation so that the school can prepare a thoughtful response, and keep your demands reasonable, while being clear about what they are.

Agree the next steps

Even if your school does ultimately agree with you about an issue, it may take time for any changes to filter through to the whole school. Improvement tends to work in cycles, and it can be bad for school culture to change a policy or teaching practice suddenly in the middle of a term. A good strategy is to agree what the short-term and long-terms steps are likely to be. This gives the school an opportunity to address the immediate concerns about your child's experience, but also invites them to think about what might happen in the long-term.

Recognise the importance of school culture

For your child's school to be effective they must establish and maintain a school culture: values, beliefs and rules that need to be applied to everyone to have any value. Any classroom issue is likely connected to the wider school culture in complicated ways. The need to maintain consistency and fairness is a really important part of how great schools achieve success. Listen to the school's reasoning and if they are willing to agree some changes, ask for reasonable adjustments within the wider school culture rather than treatment that is outside the normal conventions of the school. While you should not accept excuses when it comes to safeguarding the welfare of your child or special educational needs (see Chapter 9), it is wise to make a clear distinction between what is genuinely putting your child at risk, and what is a mere disagreement about school culture.

Example

A PARENT EFFECTIVELY COLLABORATING WITH A SCHOOL TO RESOLVE AN ISSUE

Amira is worried about the amount of homework her child's primary school is setting.

1. Amira books a meeting in with her child's teacher after school one day. Here she asks the teacher *'What is the goal of giving out this amount of homework?'* The teacher explains that this is school policy and that the homework is intended to help the child learn how to cope with secondary school, as well as supporting learning in class. Amira asks the teacher to take her through a week of homework to help understand its value.

2. At the end of the meeting Amira still feels that most of the homework being set is unnecessary, although she is starting to better understand the purpose of some of the homework in helping consolidate the learning in lessons. She feels it would be better if her child was able to focus on the relevant homework and not the rest of it. Amira asks who she can speak to at the school about the homework policy. The teacher explains that the deputy headteacher is probably the best person to speak to. She offers to arrange a meeting.

3. At the subsequent meeting, Amira makes sure she praises the aims of the homework policy but raises her concerns about the value of the homework. She talks through a couple of examples from her daughter's class. The deputy headteacher tries to reassure her of the value of the tasks, and she makes a couple of points that reassure Amira that they are thinking about the issues she has raised. However, she still thinks she and the school differ on the relevance and quantity of homework, so she asks them to consider a compromise, but asks them to go away and think about it, agreeing to think about a short-term and a long-term plan to take this forward.

4. When they meet the next week, the school suggest that the teacher could email the weekly homework through to her and she can decide if there are any homework tasks that she is going to ask her child to opt out of. Amira agrees, and says that if the teacher ever deems a piece of homework essential, she will make sure her child does it as thoroughly as possible. They agree to review the situation in a few weeks, particularly the impact it has had upon her child's learning.

What should I do next?

START A CONVERSATION WITH YOUR SCHOOL'S STAFF

Schools usually have a rich internal conversation about teaching and learning that is rarely shared with parents. This is not because of any secrecy on the part of schools, but simply because it is generally seen as a professional conversation that requires specialist knowledge and expertise to understand. Most teachers and leaders are very happy to learn that there are parents among their community who have taken time to understand the subtleties of the learning process and want to find out more about the pedagogical approaches used in the school. If you approach the teachers and school leaders in a positive, collaborative fashion and ask about their teaching and learning approaches, schools will often engage in a more sophisticated conversation with you. Here are some suggestions.

- Ask if they have a teaching and learning strategy (or a similar document) you could see. This is the internal document they use to describe how the curriculum, teaching and assessment work together to help children learn. They may not wish to share this and it is up to them whether they do, but a confident school will probably want to share what they do with you.
- Use the *Questions to ask on parents' evening* sections in the other chapters to engage with individual teachers in more detail when taking part in parental events.
- Speak to other parents about the ideas you have learnt in this book at PTA events and at the school gates.

SHARE YOUR VOICE

It is important that parents who understand the education debate can articulate their views to others. Some effective ways you can do this include the following.

- **At school.** At PTA meetings and school–parent organisations, explain what you have learnt. Be an advocate for the 'best bet' approaches outlined in this book that have the most evidence for their effectiveness.
- **On social media and blogs.** Much of the conversation about education, at both a local and national level, takes place on social media and blogs. There are a lot of educator voices but not enough from parents, and often they are talking to completely different audiences. If you want to become a voice in the debate you can.
- Download and use the **Parent Ping** app from the Apple or Android app stores. This is an app created by the Educational Intelligence group to survey parents regarding their experience of schools and their opinion on key educational issues. It provides valuable data used by journalists and policy-makers to understand what parents really think.

BECOME A GOVERNOR

One of the most powerful things that a well-informed parent can do is to join the governing board of the school. Governors are drawn from the parents of children in the school, from the wider community and from other professionals in the education sector. Typically, governors meet a few times each term and are responsible for overseeing the financial health of a school and for holding the leadership of the school to account for their results and decisions. Schools are always looking for governors to join their governing boards, particularly if they can bring professional experience that might benefit the school, such as legal or marketing expertise.

Being a governor is a serious commitment with legal obligations, and don't expect it to gain your child any special favours (in fact, if you become a governor with that expectation you may well not be the right person for the job!). However, it does give you an honest look at the reality of the school, as well as the chance to oversee major decisions that will affect the lives of your child and their peers.

For further information about becoming a school governor, contact the National Governance Association (www.nga.org.uk). To become a governor you can apply online directly to the government (www.gov.uk/become-school-college-governor). However, if you wish to apply for a specific school then it is probably best to contact that school directly.

Conclusion

The most effective parents are knowledgeable about education and approach the relationship with their child's school in a collaborative way. Reading this book was, we hope, a good start on this journey, but you will have even greater success if you continue it by starting and maintaining a productive conversation with your school and other parents, and keeping up with developments in the education debate. Show your child's school you are genuinely interested in the educational choices they're making, and use the things you have learnt in this book to understand the culture and ethos of the school. In the event of a disagreement, try to enter into a collaborative, mutually respectful conversation. Good luck.

INDEX